Ricki Ostrov

D1366096

hamlyn

headaches
and migraines

Recipes and Advice to Stop the Pain

food solutions

headaches and migraines

Recipes and Advice to Stop the Pain

food solutions

Executive Editor – Jane McIntosh
Editor – Katey Day
Art Director – Keith Martin
Art Editor – Geoff Fennell
Book Design – Birgit Eggers
Picture Research – Rosie Garai and
        Christine Juneman
Production – Lucy Woodhead

First published
in Great Britain in 2000
by Hamlyn, an imprint of
Octopus Publishing Group,
2–4 Heron Quays, Docklands,
London
E14 4JP

Copyright © 2000
Octopus Publishing Group
ISBN 0 600 59683 4

A catalogue record for this book is
available from the British Library

Printed in China

Distributed in the United States and Canada
by Sterling Publishing Co., Inc.
387 Park Avenue South, New York, NY10016–8810

introduction   p.6

chapter 1   headaches and migraines explained   p.8
             > What they are. What can go wrong.
             > Types of headaches and migraines.
             > When to visit the doctor.

chapter 2   managing headaches and migraines   p.24
             > Identifying triggers.
             > Keeping a trigger diary.
             > Avoiding common triggers, including those related to foods and
               diet, alcohol, sleeping patterns, exercise, posture and stress.
             > Steps to take to avoid an attack.

chapter 3   orthodox medicines   p.38
             > Over-the-counter preparations. What is available and how they
               work to alleviate symptoms.
             > Acute treatments.
             > Preventative drugs.

chapter 4

help from complementary therapies   p.46

> Advice on choosing and using a therapist safely.
> Herbal therapies, including Chinese and Western herbalism.
> Eastern therapies, including acupuncture, acupressure and shiatsu.
> Manipulation and massage therapies, natural therapies (such as aromatherapy), relaxation, meditation and movement therapies.

chapter 5

the role of food in headaches and migraines   p.62

> Including chemical reactions to foods as triggers.
> The role of eating patterns and nutritional deficiencies.
> Food allergies and intolerances; how to detect them.

chapter 6

exclusion recipes   p.70

> Including recipes that exclude common triggers of headaches and migraines.

chapter 7

self-help nutrition   p.94

> Recipes for breakfasts, light meals, main meals and desserts to ensure a healthy, nutritious diet.

glossary and useful addresses   p.124

index   p.126

acknowledgements   p.128

contents

RIGHT: In the mid-19th century, an electrostatic or friction machine, which sent an electric current through the body, was thought to help relieve headaches.

Headaches and migraines have been with us for thousands of years. In the Middle Ages a person with an unbearable headache or migraine might have resorted to leeches, rubbing herbs over their scalp or even having a hole drilled in their skull to release the pressure they believed was responsible for the pain. Fortunately for us, great strides have been made since then. In the latter half of the 20th century, experts have been coming to grips with the problem and **developing new and improved treatments**.

Almost all of us will suffer from the occasional headache. Yet for some people, headaches or migraines are an all-too-familiar companion. Though they are very rarely a sign of some more serious condition, constant **headaches or migraines can be disruptive and debilitating** and take their toll on both the home and work front. They can seriously affect your ability to lead a normal life.

If this sounds familiar, it's time to take some positive steps to manage your condition. Though there is as yet no cure for chronic headaches or migraines, **there are lots of ways to reduce their impact as well as lessening their frequency and severity**.

This book is designed to help you understand your problem and provide ways to help you control it more effectively,

RIGHT: Headaches and migraines can disrupt our lives, but there are many ways to relieve the pain.

FAR RIGHT: By eliminating certain foods and eating healthily we can reduce the frequency of headaches.

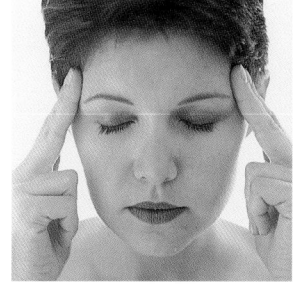

rather than letting it dominate your life. It explains the **different types of headache and migraines** so you can find out which ones are affecting you and so design a more effective treatment plan. It can help you try to pinpoint the **potential triggers** that set off your attacks, and also provides practical advice on ways to avoid them or reduce their effects.

It also details the **huge variety of treatments on offer**, from over-the-counter painkillers to medication designed specifically to help migraines. A range of complementary therapies are explained as well, so you can choose the one that best suits your needs. And because diet and nutrition play such a huge role, there are details of how to find out if certain foods are a factor, plus a selection of healthy recipes to ensure you are eating well throughout the day.

Once you have put all the information together, you will understand what factors play a role in your headaches and migraines, how to lessen their impact and see what treatments might be the most effective for you. This will allow you to **control your condition** instead of allowing it to control you.

chapter 1

A headache is one of the **most common of all medical symptoms**, and there are very few people who can claim never to have had one. For most of us it is a temporary condition and will either go of its own accord or after taking a simple painkiller. However, for some people headaches are a continual problem that can seriously disrupt their lives.

There are many different types of headaches, including the well-known migraine – a particularly intense type of headache that is thought to affect at least one person in ten. Finding out **which type of headaches you suffer from** and the possible causes and triggers can make a huge difference to controlling them satisfactorily.

This chapter explains what headaches and migraines are, the different types and their likely causes. In many instances headaches and migraines can be controlled without medical help. But we also explain **when and why you should see your doctor** and what the doctor might do to diagnose the reason for your problem. This can help put you on the road to a headache-free life, or at the very least **reduce the intensity and frequency of your attacks**.

It is simple to describe a headache – a pain in the head. However, the pain can range from a mild stabbing, throbbing or pulsating sensation that lasts a short time, to an excruciating pain that goes on for hours or days. There are many factors that can bring on a headache. Most of them are minor but occasionally a headache may be a symptom of something more serious. Common causes include illnesses such as colds and flu, faulty eyesight, drinking alcohol, tobacco or drugs (over-the-counter, prescription and recreational varieties), sinusitis, premenstrual syndrome, high blood pressure and depression. Less often headaches can be a sign of a brain tumour, meningitis or damage to the blood vessels caused by a head injury.

The pain of a headache may be felt all over the head or it may be confined to one side or part of the head. The nature of the pain can range from an aching, squeezing discomfort to a deep, pounding ache or a sharp, stabbing sensation. With migraine, in addition to the actual headache there may be accompanying or preliminary symptoms such as visual disturbances, nausea, vomiting and/or an aversion to light or sound. Unlike the common-or-garden kind of headaches, migraines tend to be associated with a specific set of trigger factors (see Chapter 2).

Although miserable and debilitating, the majority of headaches are not serious. Usually symptoms can be alleviated easily by having a short rest, going for a walk in the fresh air or taking a simple over-the-counter painkiller. However sometimes headaches are more difficult to treat. The good news is that there are many things you can do to help yourself. But in order to work out what measures would be most useful for you it helps to know a bit about why headaches develop and when it is time to see your doctor.

the head, brain and nervous system

Despite the fact that headaches are so common, doctors and scientists have yet to explain exactly what causes them. Because the whole head often feels painful you imagine that the bones of your skull and the tissues of your brain are the source of the pain when you have a headache. This is incorrect. Neither the skull nor the brain itself can feel pain because they do not contain any of the pain-sensitive nerve fibres that transmit pain messages. However, the tiny nerve endings within the blood vessels that serve the brain are extremely sensitive to changes of pressure. Pain sensations can also be transmitted to the brain by chemicals called prostaglandins from nerve endings in the skin, eyes and nose.

The soft tissues of the head consist of a covering of skin (the scalp) together with nerves, blood vessels and muscles. The bony skull which these cover consists of over 20 interlocking bones, which contain the brain, with openings for the eyes, nose and mouth. Blood is delivered to the head by

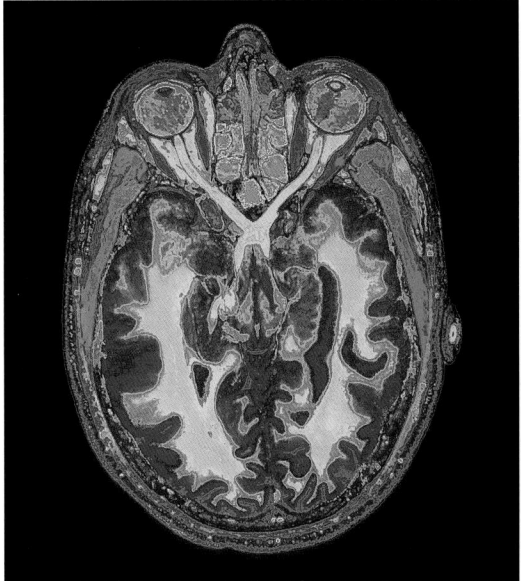

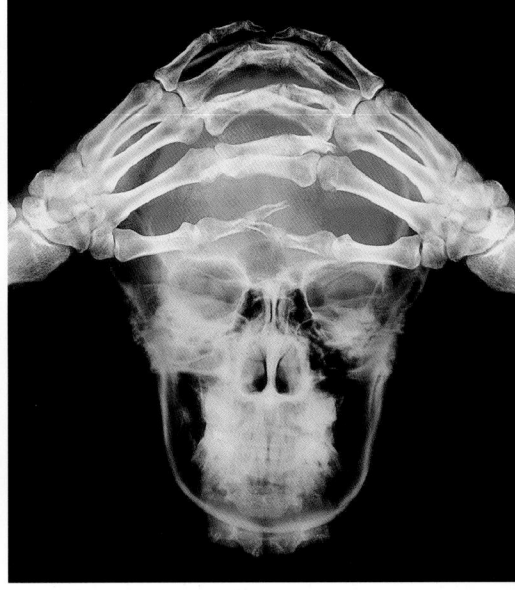

three sets of arteries: the external carotid artery which serves the face and scalp and the internal carotid and vertebral arteries which serve the brain.

The skin covering the head is also served by a complicated network of nerves, which extend across the scalp and over certain areas of the face, mouth and throat. The muscles and blood vessels of the head and at the base of the brain also contain pain-sensitive nerve endings. When you have a headache these are stimulated, making you feel pain. Many headaches are caused by expansion of the blood vessels. When the blood vessels swell they stretch the nerve endings. These so-called vascular headaches tend to produce a throbbing sensation that is intensified by physical exertion. Migraines and cluster headaches are examples of vascular headaches. Other headaches, especially the tension-type, may be caused by an increase in tension in the muscles of the scalp, leading to a more continuous tight or dull sensation or a feeling of pressure.

THE MECHANISM OF PAIN

All pain is the result of stimulation of special sensory nerve endings, known as nociceptors, which are present in various tissues throughout the body. If you feel a pain in your finger that is because nociceptors in your finger have been stimulated. When you have a headache you are responding to messages from nociceptors in your head. The stimulation may be the result of a whole host of different factors. These include physical or emotional stress, muscular tension, dilated blood vessels (vascular headache) and so on. However, no matter what the trigger, once the nociceptor is stimulated a message travels up the length of the nerve fibre to the nerve cells in your brain, telling them that your head hurts.

ABOVE LEFT: This cross-section of a head shows the eyes and nose (pink), the optic nerves (yellow) leading from the eyes and the cerebrum of the brain (yellow and purple). The nasal cavity is visible between the eyes.

ABOVE: The pink area indicates where the pain of headache is often felt – over the entire head. However, the pain does not come from the brain itself but from nerve endings within the blood vessels and muscles of the head.

**headaches
and
migraines
explained**

Pain messages are transmitted by a number of different brain chemicals, known as neurotransmitters. Some of these chemicals have a natural painkilling effect. These include hormone-like substances called endorphins, sometimes known as feel-good chemicals, that are released when we are happy or when we exercise. One theory has it that those of us who suffer from frequent or severe headaches or other types of chronic pain have lower levels of endorphins than other people.

HOW MIGRAINE OCCURS

Most headache specialists agree that migraines are a type of vascular headache, set off by the rapid widening and narrowing of blood vessel walls in the brain and head. As blood is pumped through the dilated and inflamed blood vessels, nociceptors in the blood vessel walls are irritated. This causes the sufferer to experience the throbbing pain typical of migraine.

What doctors do not really understand as yet is what causes the changes in the blood vessels to occur. Some doctors believe that migraine stems from changes in the way that blood vessels in the skull and brain react. Others argue that the problem originates in changes in the way the nervous system itself works to control the blood vessels. They claim that during a migraine attack the blood vessels are responding to changes in the brain tissue.

Many headache experts now think that people who suffer from migraines have over-reactive blood vessels. According to this view the body's nervous system responds to environmental triggers by creating a spasm in the nerve-rich blood vessels at the base of the brain. This causes the blood vessels to narrow, reducing the flow of blood to the brain. At the same time blood cells known as platelets, which are involved in blood clotting, start to clump together. As they do so they release a chemical called serotonin, which has a number of different effects. For example, serotonin in the vomiting centre in the brain is thought to be responsible for the nausea and vomiting that are characteristic symptoms of migraine. When serotonin is released during a migraine attack it narrows some blood vessels and widens others, leading to pain. Some experts believe that inherited factors affect the way serotonin is metabolized in the body.

Although headache specialists now have a clearer picture of what changes occur while a migraine attack is in progress, it is still unclear what sparks off the changes in the first place. What is known is that in people who are susceptible to migraines, one or more of a number of trigger factors can bring on an attack. If you are prone to migraines, identifying and avoiding your particular triggers is one of the most useful things you can do to control the problem.

types of headache

There are many different types of headache, all with different symptoms. Becoming aware of the different headaches will help you to plan effective treatment.

tension-type headaches

When most of us talk about having a headache these are the sorts we usually mean. The sensation of pain tends to be a steady, dull ache or feeling of pressure in the temples, forehead, the neck or back of the head and is of mild to moderate intensity. The pain is often described as being 'like a tight band' around the head or as if the head is being squeezed in a clamp or a vice.

There is still a great deal of discussion about what causes a tension headache. In the past, as the name suggests, most experts attributed it to muscular or psychological tension. Today this thinking is beginning to change. Only time will tell but in the meantime many headache specialists now prefer to use the term tension-type headache rather than tension headache. Doctors distinguish two types of tension-type headaches – episodic and chronic.

EPISODIC TENSION-TYPE HEADACHE

Most of us have experienced episodic tension-type headaches. They tend to strike randomly, often when we're going through a period of stress. An argument with your partner or the boss can often bring on this type of headache, as can getting over-tired or anxious. Physical factors such as poor posture, for example, hunching over a desk, arthritis affecting the vertebrae in the neck, problems with the muscles, bones or discs, eye-strain, especially if one eye is used more than the other, misalignment of the teeth or jaw, noise and lighting are all common triggers.

Episodic tension-type headaches are usually of short duration, lasting from half-an-hour to several days. Exercise tends not to make this type of headache worse but there may be an intolerance to light (photophobia) or noise (phonophobia). Some people seem to be more predisposed to these headaches than others and experience them recurrently. The headache is usually relieved by taking an over-the-counter painkiller, resting or having a sleep. However if you find you are getting headaches virtually every day and having to take painkillers, go and see your doctor. It may be that your headaches are chronic tension-types or are being caused by the painkillers.

ABOVE: Episodic tension-type headaches, often the result of stress, can be relieved by resting or sleeping in a quiet, darkened room.

chronic tension-type headaches

If you experience these symptoms, you may be suffering from chronic tension-type headaches:

→ Tight muscles between the head and the neck that last for days at a time over a period of months.

→ Tightness around the neck, as if your head and neck are held in a clamp.

→ A sensation of soreness, of a tightening band around your head, of pulling or of pressure.

→ The pain is continuous but not throbbing.

→ The pain mainly occurs in the forehead, temples or the back of your head and neck.

You may also experience one or more of the following:

→ Changes in sleeping patterns – either sleeping more, or insomnia or early waking.

→ Shortness of breath.

→ Digestive disturbances such as constipation or nausea.

→ Weight loss.

→ Fatigue.

→ Feelings of sadness and crying.

→ Feelings of hopelessness, guilt or despair.

→ Lack of concentration, indecisiveness and loss of interest in former pleasures.

→ Dizziness and/or palpitations.

Very occasionally a tension-type headache persists for weeks, months or even years. It is how often you get the headaches that determines whether it is episodic or chronic. Strictly speaking headache experts define a chronic tension-type headache as one that has lasted for at least 15 days per month for a minimum of 6 months. Women are more likely than men to suffer from them. As well as the symptoms described in episodic-type headaches, you may experience mild migraine-like symptoms such as throbbing, nausea and a dislike of light. The headache may vary in intensity.

Chronic tension-type headaches can be caused by stress or fatigue but are more commonly a result of physical problems or anxiety and depression. Although they are seldom disabling, they can be extremely wearing because they last for so long. If you suspect your headache is a chronic one, make an appointment with your doctor, who may prescribe preventative medication (see Chapter 3).

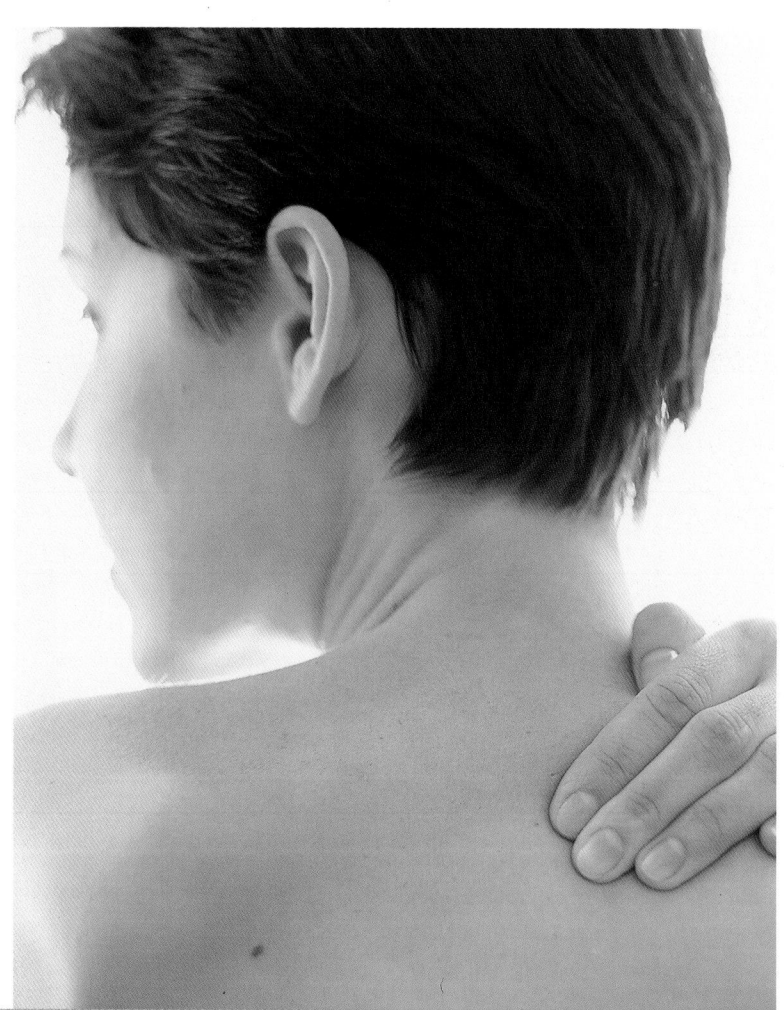

cluster headaches

These are excruciatingly painful headaches that tend to occur in groups, hence the name. Cluster headaches often come on during the night and can strike anything from once every other day to up to eight times in a single day. Most sufferers complain of one to four headaches during a cluster series. The headache may last from a quarter-of-an-hour to up to six hours. Between 'clusters' there are headache-free periods of months or years.

It is estimated that fewer than one person in ten suffers from cluster headaches. Unlike most other headaches, men tend to be more often affected than women. In fact eight out of ten sufferers are male. For some reason cluster headaches are also more likely to affect smokers and they are often precipitated by drinking alcohol.

The pain of a cluster headache has been described as the most severe and intense of any headache. Like migraine it is a vascular headache and also like migraine the pain tends to be concentrated behind one eye. The pain may begin around one eye and has been described as being 'like a nail or knife stabbing the eye'. The eye on the affected side often becomes red and watery. The eyelid may be puffy and may droop, and the pupil of the affected eye shrinks. The sufferer may also have a stuffy or runny nose and experience facial sweating. The pain of a cluster headache has been described by sufferers as being piercing, burning, throbbing or pulsating and is often so severe that in the throes of an attack many sufferers pace the floor, or sit and rock their heads and bodies.

Like migraine, cluster headaches are caused by changes in the blood vessels. However the underlying reason for the expansion of the blood vessels in cluster headaches is thought to have a different origin from that of migraines. It has been found that the levels of histamine, a chemical which triggers inflammatory reactions in the body, in the blood and urine are raised in sufferers during a cluster headache. This has led some researchers to claim that histamine plays a part, although unfortunately antihistamine medication has not been proved to be an effective form of therapy.

ABOVE: Cluster headaches are often triggered by drinking alcohol. The level of pain experienced by the sufferer is extremely high – greater than in any other type of headache.

chronic daily headache
(rebound headache)

Ironically one of the main causes of persistent daily headaches is the heavy use of over-the-counter painkillers (analgesics) used to treat other types of headaches. Excessive use of the drug ergotamine, used to treat migraine, is another cause. Most people who develop this type of

causes of rebound headaches

Your headaches may be caused by painkillers if you have been taking:

→ more than 1,000 mg of aspirin or the equivalent of another over-the-counter painkiller, more than five days a week.
→ more than three tablets per day of a compound painkiller (one containing several different ingredients) more than three days per week.
→ more than one tablet of an opioid painkiller such as codeine on more than two days per week.
→ 1 mg of ergotamine (used to prevent migraine) on more than two days per week.

BELOW: An X-ray showing the skull of a person suffering from sinusitis. The frontal sinuses (blue) above the eyes are infected.

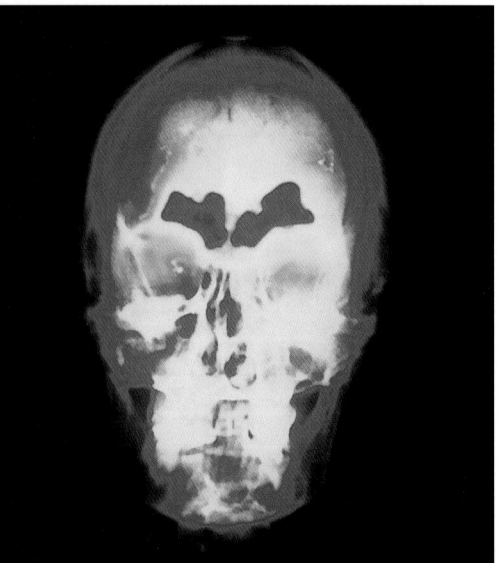

headache have been taking large daily doses of painkillers for several weeks as a treatment for another type of headache.

Puzzlingly, although the headache is not dramatically alleviated by taking a painkiller, it often flares up if the person misses a dose, hence the term 'rebound headache'. Simple painkilling drugs such as aspirin or paracetamol can be responsible for chronic daily headaches but they are more likely to be triggered by 'compound' painkillers, which contain a mixture of different ingredients such as aspirin, paracetamol and caffeine, and other painkilling drugs such as opioids. When such a headache develops from migraine, doctors sometimes call it a transformed migraine.

The main treatment is to stop taking medication completely. This will usually bring a considerable reduction in the headaches after a month or so. After this time, people with transformed migraines usually start having intermittent migraines again, while those with tension-type headaches generally get those once more.

premenstrual headache

Many women experience a headache during the premenstrual period, the week or so before the onset of menstruation. The typical premenstrual headache is often accompanied by premenstrual syndrome symptoms including fatigue, acne, joint pain, decreased urination, constipation, clumsiness, increased appetite and cravings for chocolate, salt or alcohol.

sinus headache

A sinus headache may happen when the sinuses, the bony cavities which lie in the roof and at the back of the nose, over the eyebrows and in the cheek bones on either side of the nose, become inflamed. There are many possible causes for this, including infection with the common cold, an allergic reaction such as hay fever or, in rare instances, a tumour. It is the inflammation that causes the pain.

exertion headache

Some people experience a headache that comes on during exercise or exertion. Common triggers include weight lifting and sexual activity. Other physical activities such as running upstairs can also trigger an exertion headache in some instances. The headache usually lasts for a short time and goes off gradually once you stop doing the activity which provoked it. These are called benign exertional headaches and the exact cause is unknown. However, abstaining from the activity that triggered the attacks for two or three weeks usually solves the problem. If it does not the doctor can prescribe preventive medication.

Certain medical problems such as a cerebral aneurysm (stroke), in which a blood vessel bursts in the brain, may also cause a sudden severe headache during exertion. However, unlike benign exertional headaches, those resulting from a haemorrhage last longer (usually over a day) and are usually accompanied by neurological symptoms. If the doctor suspects that a haemorrhage is the cause of a sexual or exertional headache he or she will probably order further tests such as a brain scan or lumbar puncture to try to identify the cause.

post-traumatic headache

If you have had a blow on the head severe enough to make you lose consciousness you may well develop a headache in the days and weeks following the accident or injury. In fact, about 50 per cent of people who have had such a blow will get a headache or a series of headaches. Most of these will be mild to moderate in intensity and can be relieved by taking a simple over-the-counter painkiller. Headaches are also common if your head is jerked back in a car crash, resulting in the so-called 'whiplash' effect.

Headaches following a blow or injury usually ease within a matter of weeks. However about three people in ten (or three in twenty in the case of whiplash injury) suffer from persistent headaches for many years afterwards. The International Headache Society describes these as chronic post-traumatic headaches. Research carried out in the United States suggests that three-quarters of chronic post-traumatic headaches have features of chronic tension-type headaches, while the remaining quarter have the features of naturally occurring migraine.

Although in the past a chronic post-traumatic headache has often been attributed to physical damage from an accident or injury, intriguingly there is no correlation between the severity of the accident or injury and the likelihood of the victim developing the headache. This has led some experts to suggest that it is the person's emotional reaction to the injury or accident rather than any physical damage they have suffered that has caused the headache.

sexual headache

There are two types of headache associated with sexual activity:

→ **Dull: a dull ache in the head that builds up as sexual excitement mounts. The pain fades within an hour or so.**
→ **Explosive: a sudden severe headache that strikes at or just before orgasm. The pain is often in the back of the head, on both sides. The headache usually disappears after about 15 minutes, although some last for a day or so.**

stabbing headache

Some people experience brief, stabbing pains in the head lasting anything from a fraction of a second to about ten seconds. Some sufferers describe the pain as pricking or stabbing, others say it is as if they have been struck. The pain is most often felt on one side of the head and often recurs in the same area, although it may move to other sites on the same side or on the opposite side.

Usually such headaches, known to experts as idiopathic stabbing headaches, rarely last for more than a few days. However some people may have as many as 50 a day and in some instances they can go on for months. Many of those who experience them are also prone to migraine or tension-type headaches and they tend to affect more women than men. The condition is more common in the over-40s, although sometimes children may also be affected.

headaches with serious causes

In a few instances a headache or headaches may be caused by an abnormality in the brain or skull. Such headaches are known as organic headaches. The source of the trouble may be a brain tumour (either cancerous or benign), an aneurysm (a weakness in an artery in the head which may balloon or burst), meningitis, an abscess, brain infection, cerebral haemorrhage (stroke) or encephalitis (inflammation of the brain that may be caused by some infections).

migraine

Many people use the term 'migraine' rather loosely to describe a severe headache. However migraine is a specific type of headache. Although all migraines share some typical characteristics, each individual will experience an attack in a way that is unique to them.

The pain usually begins as a dull ache, which develops into a throbbing, pulsating pain that is felt in the temples and the front and back of the head. In seven out of ten cases the headache is unilateral – that is, the pain is felt on one side of the head. Characteristically migraine is also associated with other accompanying symptoms such as nausea and/or vomiting, an

is it a tumour?

Although many people fear that a headache is caused by a brain tumour it is worth bearing in mind that fewer than one in twenty headaches are caused by a tumour. In fact, many people with a brain tumour do not suffer from headaches. If they do it is usually when the tumour is either pressing on an artery or is increasing pressure in the skull, thus irritating the nerve endings. The sort of headache caused by a tumour is likely to be sudden and intense and to get progressively worse. It is often made worse by coughing or physical exertion and may be accompanied by other symptoms such as vomiting.

ABOVE: Visual disturbances are a common symptom of migraine. These can include flashing lights, blind spots or tunnel vision.

aversion to light (photophobia) and/or noise (phonophobia). After the headache eases, the person often experiences a feeling of extreme fatigue and debilitation, a bit like having a hangover for a day or so.

Migraine usually affects adults, although children can have them too, and women are three times more likely to get them than men. In four out of five cases migraine runs in families, so if your mother or father had them you are more likely to be a sufferer yourself. The experts are still debating whether the family tendency to suffer from migraines is caused by a gene or genes, or whether it is the result of an inherited fault in the brain's pain mechanisms or in the biochemical composition of the brain.

On average, migraines strike from two to four times a month, although some sufferers may get one every few days, while others may only have one once or twice a year. The headache may strike at any time of the day or night, although it rarely wakes the person up.

There are two main types of migraine: migraine with an aura, and migraine without an aura. An aura occurs just before the headache and is characterized by a variety of symptoms, the most common of which are visual disturbances, such as seeing wavy or zig-zag lines, dots or flashing lights, tunnel vision or blind spots. You may also experience symptoms involving the nervous system such as pins and needles or numbness. These are less common than visual disturbances, but are still fairly usual.

phases of a migraine attack

There are five phases to a migraine attack, although not everyone is aware of experiencing them all.

1 THE PRODROMAL PHASE

Many sufferers are aware that they are about to develop a migraine because they feel unwell a few hours before the headache develops. There may be changes in mood, a feeling of fatigue or irritability, digestive disturbances such as constipation or diarrhoea, extreme coldness and sometimes a stiff neck. During this phase there is often a craving for particular foods, especially sweet ones such as chocolate.

2 THE AURA PHASE

Around one-third of all migraine sufferers develop an aura, a set of symptoms involving the nervous system, such as visual disturbances or numbness, before the headache begins. The aura usually comes on five minutes to half-an-hour before the headache develops and can last for up to an hour. The symptoms gradually disappear as the headache develops.

3 THE HEADACHE PHASE

This is the main part of a migraine attack. It can last from four hours to three days. The pain is severe and usually one sided, although some sufferers experience pain on both sides of the head. The pain is usually felt in the forehead or the temples. It often emanates from the back of the neck and is felt as a throbbing sensation. The pain may become more intense as the attack goes on, and is frequently aggravated by movement – anything from turning over in bed to coughing or sneezing. It is frequently accompanied by nausea, vomiting, constipation or diarrhoea, together with an aversion to bright light, noise and/or certain odours or tastes such as the smell of cigarette smoke, perfume or coffee. Loss of appetite is common during the headache phase.

4 THE RESOLUTION PHASE

During this phase the headache gradually ebbs away. At this stage many sufferers fall asleep. They may wake up to find the headache has gone.

5 THE POSTDROMAL PHASE

Once the headache has gone many sufferers feel extremely tired and drained. There may be problems concentrating, tiredness and aching muscles. A small number of sufferers feel well and energetic in the postdromal phase.

menstrual migraine

Women are three times more likely to get migraines than men, and seven out of ten women migraine sufferers get an attack before, during or immediately after a period. Some experience a migraine at ovulation, when an egg is released, around the middle of the menstrual cycle. Symptoms of menstrual migraine are similar to those of migraine without an aura, which involve a throbbing, unilateral headache, accompanied by nausea, vomiting and an aversion to light and sound. Some women may experience an aura as well. Menstrual migraines are thought to be caused by the way serotonin interacts with the female sex hormone oestrogen.

ABOVE: A high proportion of female migraine sufferers experience migraines around the time of their period, attributed to the interaction of the chemical serotonin and oestrogen.

other types of migraine

There are several other less common types of migraine including:

→ HEMIPLEGIC MIGRAINE. **A severe migraine with an aura which often begins with paralysis and/or sensory disturbances on one side of the body.**

→ OPHTHALMOPLEGIC MIGRAINE. **The pain is felt around the eyeball. It may continue for a few days to some months and the muscles around the eye may be paralysed.**

→ RETINAL MIGRAINE. **The migraine begins with temporary loss of vision in one eye. This is followed by a dull ache behind the eye that develops into a headache.**

→ BASILAR ARTERY MIGRAINE. **The migraine is accompanied by dizziness and loss of balance. There may be ringing in the ears, vomiting and difficulties with speech. It mainly affects young women and teenage girls.**

→ ABDOMINAL MIGRAINE. **The pain is felt in the abdomen and there may be nausea, vomiting and diarrhoea. Children are the most common sufferers and often go on to develop migraine proper as adults.**

→ AURA WITHOUT MIGRAINE. **Some people experience the aura without going on to develop a headache. Others experience accompanying symptoms such as nausea, vomiting and digestive disturbances.**

Try to make a note of the following information to take with you:

→ **When the headache developed.**
→ **Any factors associated with its onset, such as alcohol, stress, sunlight, a blow to the head or an accident.**
→ **How often you get headaches.**
→ **How long they last.**
→ **Whether they come and go or are continuous.**
→ **If they have become more or less frequent or severe.**
→ **If the pain of the headache is throbbing, pressing or stabbing.**
→ **If the pain is in one particular area, or more general.**
→ **If you experience associated symptoms such as nausea, vomiting, a dislike of light or noise, or a watery eye.**
→ **What treatments you have already tried, including any medication and/or complementary therapies such as acupuncture, osteopathy, herbal remedies or homoeopathy.**

visiting the doctor

If you only ever suffer from the occasional tension-type headache it is rarely necessary to consult your doctor. However if your headaches or migraines are persistent and are seriously disrupting your life, if they are especially severe, if you experience an unusual headache or if your headaches change in character, it is worth seeking medical help.

There are good reasons to see your doctor. For a start there are many medical treatments which can help control symptoms. In addition the doctor may be able to give you practical tips, support and advice on the best way to manage your headaches and/or migraine. Visiting the doctor can also reassure you that your headaches are not caused by anything serious or life-threatening.

MAKE THE MOST OF YOUR CONSULTATION

Despite the fact that headaches are so common, simply explaining to your doctor that you have a headache is of little use. You can help the doctor to help you by giving him or her as accurate a description as you possibly can of the nature of your headache, the pattern of the headaches if you experience regular headaches, and your symptoms. The more detail you can provide the better you can help your doctor to assess the nature of your headaches and what treatments are most likely to help.

WHAT THE DOCTOR MIGHT DO

There are no specific tests available for diagnosing headaches so your doctor will rely heavily on any information you provide. He or she will take a full medical history and may ask you questions about your health and lifestyle, such as your eating and drinking habits, whether you smoke, the sort of work you do and so on. You may also be asked whether there is a family history of headaches. Migraine tends to run in families, so if another member of the family is a sufferer it can offer an important clue as to the source of your problem.

The doctor may also perform a few physical checks, such as listening to your heart and lungs, measuring your blood pressure and weight, to check on your general health and to look for any clues as to what may be causing your headaches. He or she may also carry out a few simple checks such as testing your reflexes and checking the retina of your eye to see if there are any potentially serious causes affecting your nervous system. He may also take a blood sample to check for anaemia or refer you for liver or kidney function tests, or an X-ray to check whether there are any imbalances in the spine that could be a physical cause for your headaches. More rarely he or she may refer you to the hospital for a CT (computerized tomography) or MRI (magnetic resonance imaging) scan, which are specialized brain scans. Occasionally, if the doctor suspects that headaches are associated with a neurological condition such as epilepsy or with an eye condition such as glaucoma, he or she may ask for neurological or ophthalmological tests to be done.

Once the doctor has all the information needed, he or she may write a prescription for a painkiller or a more specialized drug designed for your type of headache. The doctor may also be able to offer suggestions on how to manage your headaches and reduce the number of attacks. It may take some trial and error before the doctor finds the most appropriate treatment, so be prepared to persevere. If a treatment you are prescribed is not effective do not be afraid to go back and ask for more help.

If your headaches are caused by migraines, the doctor may suggest you visit a migraine clinic. You may also consider a visit if you are unhappy with your doctor's treatment, if the headaches are associated with other medical conditions or if you are taking painkillers every day. The benefit of attending a specialist clinic is that you will have access to a team of experts who will take a holistic approach to your headaches, establishing the reasons for them and finding the most effective ways to help you.

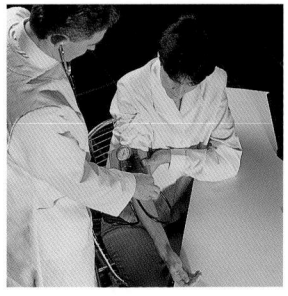

ABOVE: The doctor may carry out some simple, routine tests, such as taking your blood pressure and listening to your heart and lungs, to help pinpoint the cause of your headaches.

important reasons to see the doctor	
Although is it rare for a headache to be a symptom of anything serious, in some instances they can indicate an underlying medical condition that needs treatment. You should always seek medical attention if:	You develop a sudden, severe headache that descends like a 'bolt from the blue'.
	A headache is accompanied by loss of consciousness or alertness, confusion, blurred vision, difficulty speaking or walking, numbness, tingling or other disturbances of sensation.
	A headache is associated with convulsions or seizures, accompanied by confusion or loss of consciousness.
	It is associated with a blow on the head.
	It is accompanied by pain in the eye, ear or a purple rash.
	You develop a persistent headache and you are not someone who is normally prone to headaches.
	A child has recurrent headaches or a headache associated with a high temperature.
	You experience recurrent headaches affecting one particular part of your head such as an eye or one temple.
	You have recurrent headaches which are increasing in intensity or frequency.
	A headache is accompanied by a stiff neck, an intolerance to light and a raised temperature.
	A headache is so severe as to wake you up, or if there is a marked change in the severity of an existing headache.
	You experience a recurrent headache that is present when you wake up and is accompanied by nausea or vomiting.
	You experience any unexplained change in the nature or frequency of headaches.

Although headaches and migraines can be distressing and uncomfortable, **it helps to remember that in many instances they are self-limiting** – they will go away of their own accord without any treatment. In many cases this is because the person has learnt to deal with their headache problem by **identifying the likely causes, avoiding them when they can and taking suitable medication as soon as possible**. Learning all the likely causes of headaches and migraines may be time-consuming, but it is well worth the trouble. It can help you to feel in control, to pinpoint your personal triggers and so avoid them, and also enable you to **manage your condition more successfully**.

In this chapter you will find information on the most **common triggers of headaches and migraines** together with practical advice on what you can do to avoid or control them. You will also find hints on simple changes that you can make in your lifestyle to reduce the frequency and intensity of your headaches and migraines. Finally there is advice on what you can do to **alleviate the pain when a headache or migraine strikes** and possibly shorten its duration.

Unfair though it may seem, if you are prone to headaches and migraines there are likely to be all sorts of activities that other people can indulge in with no adverse consequences but which give you a headache. For example, a friend who is not a headache or migraine sufferer may be able to drink half a bottle of red wine, followed by several cups of coffee and go to bed late without any problems. However, bitter experience will have taught you that this will mean the inevitable pounding agony of a headache or migraine the next day.

Over the years headache and migraine experts have identified certain factors that are common causes of headaches and migraines. These factors, such as specific foods and drinks, habits or aspects of the environment, are known as triggers. Although the part played by them is most marked in migraines, other headaches such as tension-type headaches or cluster headaches are also sparked off by many of the same triggers. Many experts believe that the brains of people who experience headaches and migraines are especially sensitive to the effects of external stimulation.

identify your triggers

The first step is to identify what sets off your headaches or migraines. Becoming aware of your own personal trigger factors and doing what you can to eliminate or control them will help you reduce the number of your headaches and/or decrease their severity.

Everyone is unique so you are likely to find that the factors that trigger your headaches or migraines are different to those affecting other people. Often those who are prone to migraines find that they need a combination of triggers to bring on an attack.

Another point is that some triggers will affect you more than others. For example, a change in barometric pressure may have no effect on you whatsoever, while it is virtually guaranteed to bring on a migraine for somebody else. To complicate matters further, triggers may vary from one attack to the next. For instance, sometimes you may be able to eat blue cheese without a problem while at other times it brings on an attack. What is more, your personal triggers may change over a period of time.

TOP: Being in a smoky atmosphere in a bar or at a party and drinking alcohol are potential triggers for migraines in many sufferers.

ABOVE: Oriental food is a common cause of migraine. Keep a note in your trigger diary to help identify which foods are triggers for you.

KEEP A TRIGGER DIARY

One of the most effective ways to identify your own triggers is to keep a diary of your headaches and migraines with a note of any associated trigger factors. Not only will such a record help you pinpoint the pattern of your attacks and identify your triggers, it will also help your doctor, if you seek medical help, to reach a more accurate diagnosis. You will probably know some of the things that trigger your headaches. However keeping a diary can help you to identify which ones are most significant and indicate how many triggers you need to set off a migraine or headache.

keeping a trigger diary

Keeping a trigger diary is easy to do. Use your diary or buy a special notebook
for the purpose and keep this by your bed, in your handbag or briefcase or in an
easy-to-find spot in your house. Every time you experience a headache or migraine
attack make a note of it and make a record of the following information:

→ The date and time of any headaches or migraine attacks.

→ Details of the specific symptoms.

→ The severity of the symptoms.

→ How the symptoms progressed.

→ What treatment you took, if any, and whether it had any effect.

→ How long the attack lasted.

→ How you knew when it was over.

At the same time, either in the same notebook or diary or on a separate sheet of
paper, keep a record of potential triggers you have encountered or experienced.
This should include details of:

→ What you ate and drank.

→ When you went to sleep and when you woke.

→ The weather.

→ Your travel activities.

→ Any exercise you took.

→ Your mood.

→ Any work or social activities or events.

→ Any medications you took, including over-the-counter,
   prescribed or herbal, homeopathic or nutritional.

→ Any relevant details about your environment, for example
   going to a party and being in a smoky atmosphere.

→ If you are a woman, the dates of your menstrual periods and
   any symptoms associated with premenstrual syndrome (PMS)
   such as swollen, tender breasts, irritability or food cravings.

Some people find it easier to make a chart with a list of common triggers on
top and dates down the side and tick each one they are exposed to at the end
of each day. This makes it simpler to spot if there is any identifiable pattern.

avoiding common triggers

There are many common triggers, and it is likely that at least one of the following may affect you. Some are easier to keep track of and avoid, such as certain foods and drinks, smoking and getting enough sleep. Others, however, are more difficult to control, such as pregnancy, stress or weather patterns, but it is still possible to reduce the effects these triggers may have, which in turn may help to reduce the frequency or severity of your attacks.

food and diet

At least three out of ten migraine attacks are said to be linked to specific foods and drinks. Chocolate, cheese and citrus fruits are among the most common causes. Other possibilities include peanuts; chicken livers; pickles; broad beans, peas and lentils; Chinese, Thai, Vietnamese and other Oriental foods; and dishes and processed meats such as frankfurters, bacon, ham and pepperoni.

The experts are not quite sure why certain foods trigger headaches. Some believe it could be an allergic reaction to a particular food. Some point to certain chemicals or ingredients in foods that may affect the blood vessels. Others say that it is not actually food itself that causes an attack, arguing that during the anticipatory phase of a migraine (the prodromal phase) the sufferer craves a particular food, such as chocolate, and then attributes the headache to the food.

TAKING CONTROL

Whatever the truth, you may be able to minimize the number of your attacks by avoiding these foods. This should be done systematically by leaving out foods and introducing them again after a period of time to check whether they do cause a headache or migraine. Because the process is complicated, it is best done under medical supervision. For further details on food and diet, see Chapter 5.

BELOW: Citrus fruit, such as lemons and limes, are among the most potent food triggers for migraines. The other most common culprits are chocolate and cheese.

alcohol

Alcoholic drinks are common triggers of all sorts of headaches. Migraine is perhaps the best known, but alcohol also frequently triggers a headache during a cluster series and, of course, it is also implicated in 'hangover' headaches. Various reasons have been suggested to explain why alcohol brings on a headache. Some experts blame substances found in the alcohol such as flavonoids, nutrients found in the skins of black and red grapes, or congeners, chemicals used in processing wine. In hangover headaches dehydration of the tissues induced by alcohol almost certainly plays a part, as well as chemical by-products of alcohol produced as it is broken down by the system, such as acetone.

TAKING CONTROL

You may find that certain types of alcohol are particular culprits, for example red wine and spirits like brandy and whisky are commonly linked to migraine. Alternatively there may be certain methods of production that are linked to headaches, for example you may find that wines matured in oak barrels, such as some Chardonnays, cause you problems. Quantity may also determine whether or not someone gets a headache. You may be able to drink one glass of red wine without getting a headache or migraine but find that two or more glasses tip the balance. In the case of migraines other factors are often implicated too. You may be able to tolerate the occasional glass of red wine, provided you are careful to avoid other triggers.

Using your trigger diary you can gain some insight into the types of alcohol and patterns of consumption that are especially associated with your headaches or migraines. Once you have done so you can decide to avoid the type of alcohol and/or modify your drinking habits. For example you may find that avoiding drinking on an empty stomach and confining your alcohol intake to mealtimes helps to buffer the effects of alcohol and prevents a headache.

TOP: Spirits such as brandy and whisky can cause migraines in many sufferers, but gin and vodka seem to be less of a problem.

ABOVE: Red wine is another common trigger, but you may find you can drink a small quantity of a certain type without an attack.

eating patterns

As well as food itself, your eating habits may also be linked to your headaches and migraines. Skipping meals, not eating enough or consciously cutting down because you are dieting are all extremely

common triggers both of tension-type headaches and migraines. This is thought to be due to low blood sugar. Whenever you eat something the glucose levels in your blood rise. Your body draws on this glucose supply to provide energy. After a period of time the glucose levels fall again. If you eat something the blood sugar levels start to rise again, but if you skip a meal they continue to fall.

The process by which blood sugar levels are controlled is extremely complicated. However some people seem to be especially sensitive to fluctuations in their blood sugar. If their blood sugar is low, as it is when you are hungry or have missed a meal or after strenuous exercise, a headache or migraine may develop.

TAKING CONTROL

Many people find that eating small, regular meals helps to avoid the peaks and troughs in their blood sugar levels that can bring on a headache. Try to eat three meals a day plus a couple of healthy snacks. If you think you are likely to miss a meal for any reason, pack a snack such as a banana or a sandwich to tide you over.

hormonal changes

Many women find that headaches and migraine attacks are related to their reproductive cycle and occur at times of hormonal fluctuation such as before and during menstruation, during the withdrawal week when taking the combined contraceptive pill, during pregnancy, after the menopause or when they are on HRT (hormone replacement therapy).

TOP: Low blood sugar levels can be the every-day cause of both tension-type headaches and migraines, so it is important not to miss meals. Take healthy carbohydrate-rich snacks with you when you are on the move.

ABOVE: Breakfast is the most important meal of the day since your blood sugar levels need to be replenished after the long night.

MENSTRUATION

A headache is a common symptom of PMS during the week or so before menstruation begins and many women get headaches during the first few days of menstruation too. True 'menstrual migraines' are defined as migraines that occur only at the time of menstruation. They begin within two days of a period starting and may last up to the end of the third day of the menstrual flow. In fact only a small percentage of migraines fall within this strict definition.

Nevertheless, many women who get headaches and migraines at other times of the month also have migraines before or during menstruation. These are described as menstrually related migraines. The distinction is significant because it is thought that the causes are different in each instance. In the case of true menstrual migraines the cause is thought to be the fall in the female sex hormone oestrogen that triggers the migraine. It could be that women who experience this are abnormally sensitive to their own natural hormonal fluctuations. In the case of menstrually related migraines it is clear that hormonal changes are just one of a number of other trigger factors.

TAKING CONTROL

If you suspect your headaches or migraines are related to your menstrual cycle, you will need to be diligent about keeping track of your potential triggers. Analyse your trigger diary and try to avoid your triggers before and during menstruation. This may involve changing your eating habits, avoiding certain foods, and paying special attention to your health. If the headaches or migraines are particularly troublesome, talk to your doctor about the possibility of taking medication at this time.

THE CONTRACEPTIVE PILL

Some women find that going on the contraceptive pill causes their headaches and migraine attacks to become more frequent and severe. Others find the opposite. The majority find that taking the pill has no effect one way or the other.

The combined pill, as it is known, contains two female sex hormones, oestrogen and progestogen. Most doctors agree that it is safe to take the combined pill if you get migraines without an aura. However it is generally felt that women who suffer from migraines with an aura or whose migraine changes to one with an aura when they go on the pill should not continue taking the combined pill.

TAKING CONTROL

If your trigger diary reveals that the pattern or type of migraine attacks have changed since you started taking the pill have a word with your doctor. It could be that you need to change to the progestogen-only pill, which does not contain oestrogen, or consider using an alternative contraceptive method.

PREGNANCY

During early pregnancy headaches and migraines may be associated with low blood sugar triggered by food aversions, or the nausea and vomiting that are common during the first 12 weeks of pregnancy. Many women

BELOW: While some develop headaches and migraines during pregnancy, particularly in the very early stages, regular sufferers may find that their migraines are less frequent.

the oestrogen factor

No one is quite certain what relationship the female sex hormone oestrogen has to headaches and migraines. What is known is that higher levels of oestrogen trigger increases in serotonin, the brain chemical, which is thought to play a crucial part in causing migraine. When oestrogen levels fall – for example in the second half of the menstrual cycle or in the pill-free week – serotonin levels also drop. This may trigger a migraine due to the action of serotonin on the blood vessels. But this is not the full story. If it were, oestrogen supplements ought to cure migraines in all women who suffer from menstrual migraines or migraines in the pill-free week. Current research is attempting to determine the various factors involved.

BELOW: Hormonal changes caused by the menopause can trigger migraine attacks.

find that their migraines become less frequent or severe during pregnancy. However, about 15–20 per cent of pregnant women get migraines. One or two per cent of women have migraines for the first time during pregnancy or find that the type of migraine they get changes, for example they may begin to experience an aura.

During late pregnancy a severe headache, especially combined with visual disturbances, can be a symptom of late stage pre-eclamptic toxaemia (PET), a disease affecting the placenta. Left untreated it can cause seizures and the death of both the mother and the baby. The first signs of pre-eclampsia are raised blood pressure, together with protein in the urine and swelling of the tissues. Regular checks are carried out throughout pregnancy to pick up any potential signs of pre-eclampsia.

TAKING CONTROL

Eating little and often can help combat the dips in blood sugar that may trigger a headache or migraine. Taking time to rest and relax can help too. If you take medication for your headaches or migraines check with your doctor, before you conceive, that it is safe to continue using them during pregnancy. Always report any severe headache immediately to your doctor.

MENOPAUSE

Non-migrainous headaches are quite common at the menopause, although it is not known exactly why. It could be partly hormonal change combined with other factors such as insomnia, stress and tension. Studies looking at migraine have found that just under half of women experience more severe attacks during the menopause. The good news is that by and large migraines tend to wane after the menopause. In fact both men and women aged over 55 experience fewer migraines. Some women who are prescribed hormone replacement therapy (HRT) may find that the treatment worsens their migraines, although others find the opposite.

TAKING CONTROL

Your trigger diary can help identify if headaches and migraines are associated with the menopause itself or with associated factors such as stress, sleeplessness and so on. If they are, it is worth having a word with your doctor. If HRT seems to exacerbate your migraines talk to your doctor about trying a different preparation. There are a wide number of different types available nowadays and with a bit of trial and error it is usually possible to find one that suits you.

sleeping patterns

Many headache and migraine sufferers find that changes in their sleeping habits – from going on holiday, doing shift work, going to bed late, having to get up early or having a lie-in – can trigger an attack. Insomnia too, when you find it hard to get to sleep at night or drop off only to wake up and be unable to get back to sleep, is another trigger for many people. This is curious because sleep is often a cure for an acute headache or migraine. It is not known exactly why having too much or too little sleep can trigger headaches. If you are unsure whether your sleeping patterns are playing a part in your headaches or migraines your trigger diary should help you. Alternatively you can try deliberately breaking your regular sleeping patterns by sleeping in or staying up late to see whether this triggers a headache or a migraine.

TAKING CONTROL

If you do find that your headaches or migraines are linked to your sleeping habits try to keep to a regular routine, going to bed and getting up at the same time each day – even at weekends and when you go away on holiday. If you are going on holiday to somewhere where the time is an hour or so different, try adjusting your clock by about 15 minutes per day to allow your body clock time to adjust to the new time. If you are crossing time zones you may have to accept that you will develop a headache when you arrive at your destination. However you may be able to reduce the chances of one occurring by switching to the new time and having your meals and sleeping at the time it will be in the country of your destination the minute you board the aeroplane.

exercise and exertion

Although exercising is a good way to help combat everyday stress and disperse the stress hormones that may be involved in triggering a headache or migraine, over-exercising can bring on an attack. One reason may be muscle strain brought about by overdoing certain activities or by poor posture when exercising. Examples of activities that may bring on a headache include lifting heavy weights at the gym, playing a strenuous game of tennis or pulling up the sail if you go windsurfing. All these activities can put a strain on your back and neck, which in turn can trigger a headache or migraine. Exertion and exercise also lower your blood sugar as the body draws on glucose from the blood for energy – another headache trigger.

BELOW: Changes in sleeping patterns can trigger a headache or migraine, so note the times you go to bed and get up in your trigger diary to see whether this is a factor for you.

BELOW: To avoid triggering a headache, approach any new physical activity with care without pushing yourself. Eat a snack beforehand to maintain your blood sugar level.

ABOVE: Drink plenty of liquids before and after exercising to replace lost fluids and prevent dehydration, which could bring on a headache.

If you begin an exercise programme start slowly and build up gradually. Do not over-exert yourself. If you join a gym take advantage of any fitness assessments that may be offered so your programme is tailored to your individual needs, and ensure that you learn to perform each exercise correctly. Eat a carbohydrate-rich meal or snack an hour or so before you exercise to help keep your blood sugar levels stable. Make sure you drink plenty of water to make up for lost fluids. A banana or light carbohydrate snack eaten after exercising can help maintain your blood sugar levels.

posture

The way you hold yourself can play a big part in headaches and migraine. The spinal cord, which contains all the nerves running from your head to the rest of the body, runs from the head to the base of your back and is protected by the bones of your spinal column (the vertebrae). Upper and lower back problems, holding yourself awkwardly, sitting poorly at home or at work or lying in an awkward position in bed, can all put pressure on the nerves of the spinal cord and trigger a headache or a migraine. Injury to the back or neck can have a similar effect as can bending, straining or lifting a heavy object, such as carrying heavy shopping bags.

Look carefully at the way you stand and sit at work, rest and play. Look at your work station and make sure your chair is the correct height: your feet should be flat on the floor and your thighs at right angles to your back. When carrying shopping try to distribute the weight equally between two bags (one in each hand) or carry the shopping in a rucksack – do not carry it over one shoulder, which can throw off your posture and balance. Instead, use both straps and position the rucksack against the middle of your back.

environmental factors

Headache and migraine sufferers tend to be extremely sensitive to changes in their external environment. All sorts of factors from a change in the weather to being in a smoky atmosphere or travelling to a higher altitude can trigger an attack. It is not known exactly why some people are more sensitive than others to these changes.

However in the case of migraines it is thought that weather changes may trigger an attack by disturbing the body's biochemical balance. Dry, dusty atmospheres, for example, are thought to cause electrically charged dust particles to be released. If inhaled these can stimulate the production of chemicals that act on the blood vessels. Winds and stormy weather may have a similar effect. Changes in barometric pressure can trigger migraines, too, as can changes in pressure brought about by flying, diving or travelling to a high altitude. In this case it is thought that the fall in oxygen levels in the bloodstream causes the arteries in the scalp to expand in order to compensate for loss of oxygen.

In fact, virtually anything affecting your senses can bring on a headache or a migraine if you are susceptible. Many headache and migraine sufferers are especially sensitive to light and glare. Anything from sunlight reflected off snow or water to the flickering from a television screen or sleeping with the light on may cause a headache. Smells, fumes and vapours can have an effect too. Common culprits are tobacco smoke, car fumes or fumes from a central-heating boiler in a poorly ventilated room or building. (Incidentally, smokers are more likely to experience cluster headaches.) Loud noises such as music from an upstairs flat or the next-door house may precipitate a headache or migraine too, possibly because they trigger muscle tension and the release of stress hormones.

TAKING CONTROL

Unfortunately our external environment is one of the things over which we have the least control. There are a few obvious things you can do in your own home, like ensuring you have your central heating boiler checked every year, opening windows, avoiding smoky atmospheres, trying to keep noise levels down and using black-out blinds or curtains if light is a problem when you sleep. However, apart from these measures there may be little you can do. The good news is that identifying factors in your environment that you know trigger a headache or migraine attack can help you to anticipate when one is likely to strike. You can then take pre-emptive action, for instance taking a painkiller, which may stop the attack from developing or at least lessen its severity.

stress and tension

Physical and emotional stress and tension are key factors in both migraines and tension-type headaches, so much so that many experts believe that headache and migraine sufferers react more readily than

BELOW: Stress, caused by starting a new job for example, is thought to be a major cause of headaches and migraines due to the effects of adrenaline on muscles and blood vessels.

other people to stress. In fact one of the reasons environmental changes cause headaches and migraine could be because they involve stress.

But what exactly is stress and how can it cause a headache? Whenever you encounter a new situation – anything from starting a new job or having an argument – your body has to adapt both physically and mentally. In order to do so it sends out stress hormones, such as adrenaline, chemical messengers which put your body on red alert. This is known as the stress response. It is designed to enable your body to cope with the new situation either by running away or facing up to it – a phenomenon commonly known as the 'fight or flight' reaction.

Adrenaline and other stress hormones affect virtually every single one of the body's organs and tissues. One of the most significant effects, where headaches and migraines are concerned, is that they cause changes in the width of the blood vessels which are closely linked to migraine. Another effect is that the muscles become tense as the body prepares to flee or fight off the attack. This muscle tension exacerbates pain and can increase the severity of a headache. After the stress has passed there is often a period of relaxation during which the blood vessels and muscles relax and widen. Strangely enough this, too, can trigger a headache. In fact it is one reason why headache and migraine sufferers experience weekend headaches or why a headache often comes on after a period of stress.

As well as these quantifiable psychological and physical reactions there are often other factors that combine to make certain environmental changes sure-fire headache triggers. Travel, for example, is a common trigger of both headaches and migraines. Travelling frequently involves changes in sleeping patterns, the daily routine and diet – all independent trigger factors for headaches and migraine – as well as muscular tension from sitting in a cramped position in a plane, bus, train or car, or being jarred by the motion of the vehicle.

TAKING CONTROL

It is impossible – and indeed undesirable – to avoid all stress. However, you can minimize its adverse impact by anticipating stressful events and planning for them. During a period of stress look after yourself and try to keep your daily routine regular. Make sure you have a good breakfast and take the time to eat proper meals. Try to make sure you get enough sleep. Learn stress management techniques: there are plenty of books, videos and tapes available to help you. It may also help to learn some relaxation exercises or techniques such as yoga, meditation or T'ai chi. And get some exercise. This helps to release endorphins, the body's own painkilling hormones. It also helps to disperse stress hormones such as adrenaline.

BELOW: Maintaining a routine of nourishing meals and adequate sleep can help to manage stress. Relaxation techniques, such as meditation, work well for many people.

**managing
headaches
and
migraines**

during an attack
Even with the best
will in the world,
some headaches
and migraines are
unavoidable. But
there are steps
you can take if you
develop a headache
or realize that
a migraine is on
the horizon.

→ **Start early and tackle a headache or impending migraine straightaway.** This can help thwart an attack or make it less severe. Once any sort of pain has taken hold it is much more difficult to control. What is more, once a migraine has set in, the digestive system shuts down making it impossible for you to absorb anything you take by mouth. There are a number of different preparations on the market for headaches and migraines, though it may take some trial and error before you find out which ones work best for you (see Chapter 3).

→ **Try to eat something.** If low blood sugar is the culprit this simple step may be enough to ward off your headache. If you are in the throes of a migraine attack eating something bland such as a piece of toast or a plain biscuit can also help alleviate any nausea. If you are unfortunate enough to be sick, this will be less uncomfortable than vomiting on an empty stomach. But do not force yourself to eat if you have lost your appetite.

→ **Take a little gentle exercise.** Sometimes stopping what you are doing and going for a short walk can help banish a headache or incipient migraine. This often works well with tension-type headaches that have been brought on by sitting for too long in one position.

→ **Open a window.** Letting in some fresh air can help reduce headaches and migraines that are made worse by stuffy atmospheres.

→ **Rest and relax.** Ideally, once a headache or migraine has really set in you should stop what you are doing and rest in a quiet, darkened room. If you are able to sleep you may find that your headache or migraine is considerably eased or even disappears completely once you wake up.

→ **Get comfortable.** This may be difficult, but take some steps to make yourself as comfortable as possible when pain strikes. It might help to wrap up warmly, and if light bothers you draw the curtains or wear an eye mask. If noise is a problem use ear plugs.

→ **Take it easy.** If a headache or migraine strikes at work or when you are busy, resting may not be an option. In this case try to do something undemanding. Not only does concentrating often involve muscle tension, which can worsen pain, but you will also find it harder to focus your attention. As soon as you can, try to rest until the attack has passed.

→ **Apply a compress.** Many sufferers find that applying a hot or cold compress to the most painful area brings relief. Use a hot-water bottle or, if your headache improves with the application of something cold, use an ice pack, a specially designed mask to wear over the eyes, or even a packet of frozen peas (wrapped in a towel to avoid damaging the skin).

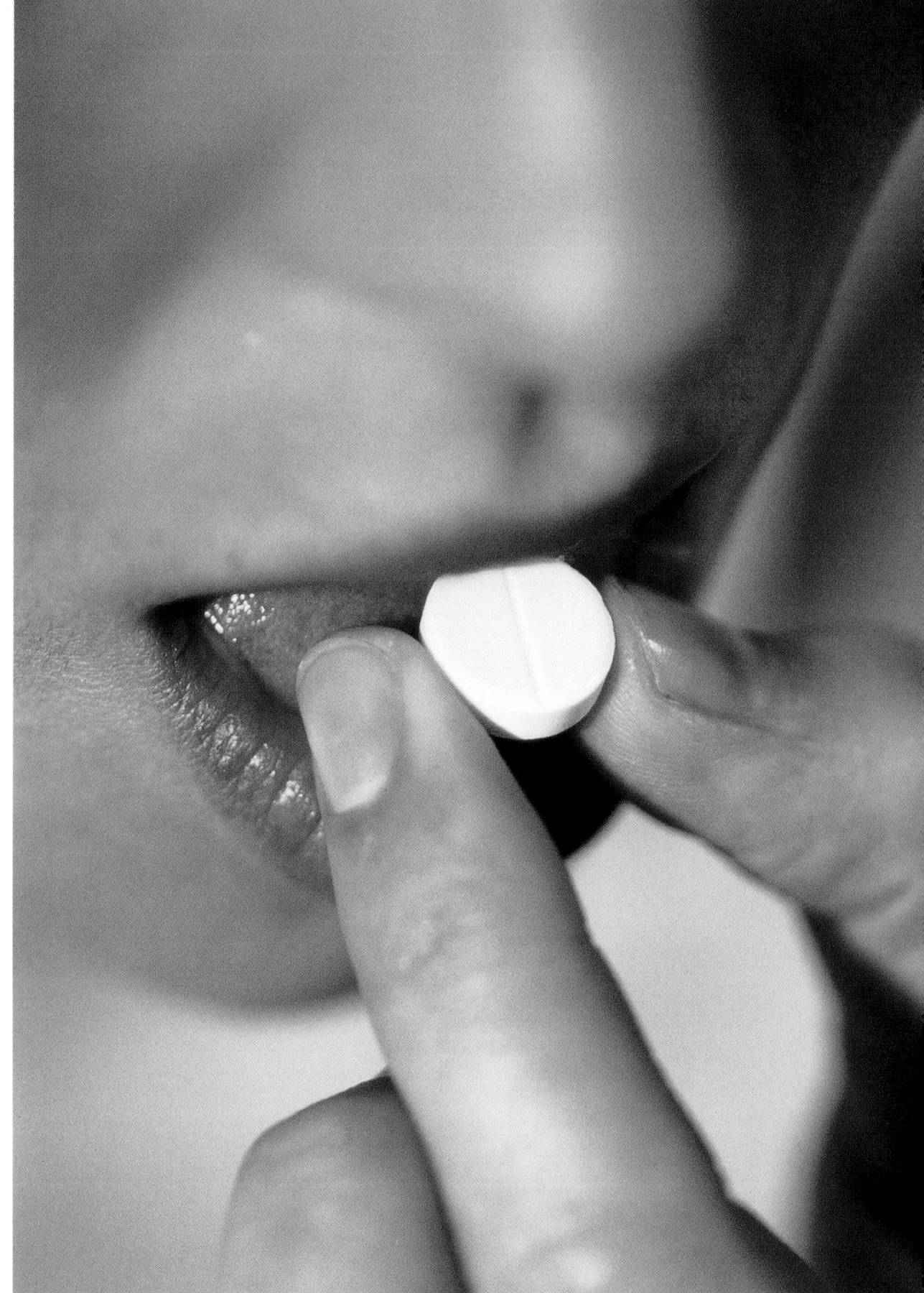

chapter 3

There is a huge range of **painkilling medicines to help ease the agony of headaches and migraines**. There are also special medicines available to reduce the nausea and vomiting that are often symptoms of a migraine attack. Some of these medications can be purchased over the counter, while others are only available on prescription. None of the medications will cure chronic headaches or migraines: **most are intended to reduce the pain and accompanying symptoms** and are taken immediately these begin, **others act as a preventative measure** and are taken regularly to reduce the frequency or severity of attacks. With the huge choice on offer these days, it is likely that you will be able to find one that suits you and eases your symptoms and discomfort.

It may take some trial and error before you find out which types of medicines work best for you. If you have any problems or find that the medicines do not do their job effectively, **discuss the situation with your doctor**, who may be able to recommend a different formulation or a stronger medication. Always let your doctor know if you have any problems, difficulties or side effects with any medication you are taking – including over-the-counter remedies as well as prescription medicines.

over-the-counter preparations

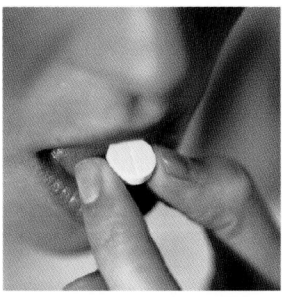

orthodox
medicines

Over-the-counter medicines are used to help reduce the pain of headaches and migraines. Called analgesics, or painkillers, the most common types contain aspirin, paracetamol, ibuprofen or a combination of more than one of these drugs together with other ingredients, such as small doses of more powerful analgesics.

The type of over-the-counter painkiller you choose can depend on a number of factors, including your overall health and whether you are on any other medicines. For example, aspirin should be avoided by pregnant women, people suffering from bleeding disorders or peptic ulcers, and should never be given to children younger than 12. The best thing is to talk to your doctor or pharmacist about which painkiller would be most suitable for you.

ASPIRIN

Aspirin is one of the oldest and most popular forms of over-the-counter analgesic. It has been used for many years to relieve the pain of headaches and migraines, and works in a number of ways. First it is an analgesic, and so reduces the pain. Second, it blocks or reduces inflammation. It does this in part by blocking or reducing the production of chemicals called prostaglandins. It also helps to reduce the ability of platelets to stick together. This is important in the treatment of migraine, as platelets stick together which causes them to release serotonin into the bloodstream, which can lead to effects on the blood vessels and cause migraine.

Aspirin is available in a variety of formulations, primarily tablets and capsules. Some of these are coated to make them gentler on the stomach and digestive tract and therefore less likely to cause bleeding. You can also buy soluble forms – these are dissolved in water and work more quickly but are not any easier on the digestive tract.

WATCHPOINT

Aspirin has some drawbacks. It can cause irritation of the lining of the digestive tract, which can lead to internal bleeding, and so is unsuitable for those with peptic ulcers or other digestive problems. Because it alters the blood-clotting mechanisms, it should not be used by anyone with a bleeding disorder. Aspirin is also unsuitable for use during pregnancy, for those with asthma, long-term kidney or liver problems, or for children under the age of 12.

PARACETAMOL

A different form of analgesic, paracetamol is thought to work by reducing the production of prostaglandins in the brain. It is useful for treating everyday aches and pains such as headaches, particularly if the pain is mild to moderate. Paracetamol is one of the safest over-the-counter analgesics when taken correctly. It does not irritate the stomach and allergic reactions are rare. It is also safe for occasional use in pregnancy. It is a good alternative to aspirin for people with peptic ulcers or those who are allergic to aspirin. Paracetamol comes in a variety of forms, including tablets, capsules and liquids.

WATCHPOINT

Paracetamol should not be taken by anyone with long-term kidney or liver problems. An overdose is very dangerous and capable of causing serious damage to the liver and kidneys. Always follow the dosage recommendations, and be especially careful if you are taking other medications, for instance cold remedies. These often contain paracetamol and you may get more than the recommended dose if you take more than one remedy at the same time.

You should also remember that overuse of analgesics can lead to 'rebound' headaches. This is especially true if the medicine you take contains caffeine, which helps speed up the efficacy of other ingredients. If you find you are taking analgesics more than a few days a week, you may be susceptible to rebound headaches.

To get the most out of your medicine, you should take the painkillers as early in the attack as possible. If you find that these medicines are not effective, or not as effective as they once were, it's time to see your doctor about other options. Always follow the instructions on the bottle or packaging and do not take more than the recommended dose.

Discuss which painkiller is best for you with your doctor or pharmacist.

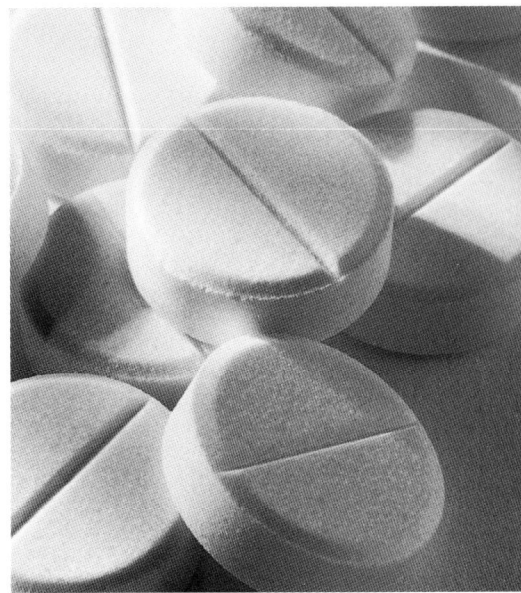

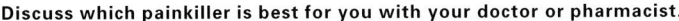

IBUPROFEN

Ibuprofen is one of a type of medicines known as non-steroidal anti-inflammatory drugs, or NSAIDs. These are related to aspirin and can relieve both pain and inflammation by blocking or reducing the production of prostaglandins. For these reasons it may prove useful in cases of headaches and migraines causing mild to moderate pain.

However, like aspirin, ibuprofen can irritate the stomach lining so is not usually suitable for those who have peptic ulcers or other disorders of the digestive tract, nor is it suitable for use during pregnancy.

WATCHPOINT

Ibuprofen should not be used by anyone with long-term kidney problems, high blood pressure, asthma or peptic ulcers or other disorders of the digestive tract. It should also be avoided by anyone who has had an allergic reaction to aspirin. A reduced dose may be necessary for children or the elderly.

CODEINE

Not available on its own without a prescription, codeine is a common ingredient in many combination or compound analgesics. It has mild narcotic effects, and is good for relieving mild to moderate headache or migraine pain.

WATCHPOINT

Codeine is a narcotic analgesic, and has a sedative effect on the nervous system. It can lead to drowsiness so anyone taking a preparation containing codeine should be careful when driving or operating heavy machinery. It should not be used without medical advice by anyone with long-term kidney or liver problems, lung disorders such as asthma or bronchitis, or those taking other medications. It should be used with extreme caution during pregnancy and breastfeeding. Because there is a risk of dependency, codeine should be used only for short periods of time to relieve specific symptoms.

acute treatments

Medicines that are taken only during attacks are often known as acute treatments and include analgesics you can buy without a prescription. But for many sufferers these over-the-counter painkillers are not strong enough or, over time, become less effective. It is not safe to continue to increase the dose in the hopes of getting relief from your pain. This is the time to discuss the situation with your doctor, who has a much wider range of medications available.

The two main drugs used for preventing the pain of migraine, and occasionally cluster headaches, do not have the same actions as painkillers. Instead, they are thought to help relieve the pain of a migraine or cluster headache by narrowing the dilated blood vessels.

RIGHT: Over-the-counter medicines give relief by dulling the pain, but other drugs that work in different ways are only available on prescription.

ERGOTAMINE

This drug has been used successfully for many years to prevent and treat the pain of migraine headaches. It is called a vasoconstrictor and works by narrowing the dilated blood vessels around the skull. Ergotamine is usually recommended for those for whom other analgesics or anti-inflammatory drugs do not work.

Ergotamine is available in a number of different formulations, including tablets, inhalers and suppositories. Suppositories are useful for those whose migraines involve vomiting and so cannot keep tablets down. There is also a type of tablet that is placed under the tongue and absorbed into the bloodstream, and an inhaler for rapid relief of migraine. Ergotamine is most effective when taken at the first sign of an impending migraine.

WATCHPOINT

Because ergotamine narrows the blood vessels throughout the body, not just the brain, it should not be used by those with circulatory disorders. If you notice any tingling, numbness or coldness in your fingers and toes, stop taking the drug and talk to your doctor. It could be that the drug is causing over-constriction in other blood vessels. Other side effects include nausea, vomiting and drowsiness, so it can be difficult to tell whether the symptoms are caused by the attack or by the drug. Ergotamine should not be used by children, pregnant or breastfeeding women, or by people with kidney or liver disorders or severely high blood pressure.

SUMATRIPTAN

Sumatriptan is a newer type of drug that was developed specifically for the treatment of migraine and cluster headaches. In some ways it works in a similar fashion to ergotamine, by reducing the size of the swollen blood vessels, but it only affects the cranial blood vessels – those in the brain – rather than blood vessels throughout the body. Its other important action is to inhibit the effects of serotonin (also known as 5-HT), which can help stop a migraine or cluster headache from progressing.

Sumatriptan is available as a tablet, a pre-filled self-injectable syringe, a tablet, and as a nasal spray. The self-injectable syringe is the form most often recommended for treatment of cluster headaches.

WATCHPOINT

Sumatriptan can cause side effects including sudden wheeziness, fluttering or tightness in the chest, swelling of the eyelids, face or lips, or a skin rash, all of which can indicate an allergic reaction to the medicine. As with ergotamine, you may feel tired or dizzy, or suffer from nausea or vomiting. It can be difficult to determine if these symptoms are due to the migraine or the medication. Sumatriptan is not suitable for those who are pregnant or breastfeeding, or suffering from certain circulatory and heart disorders.

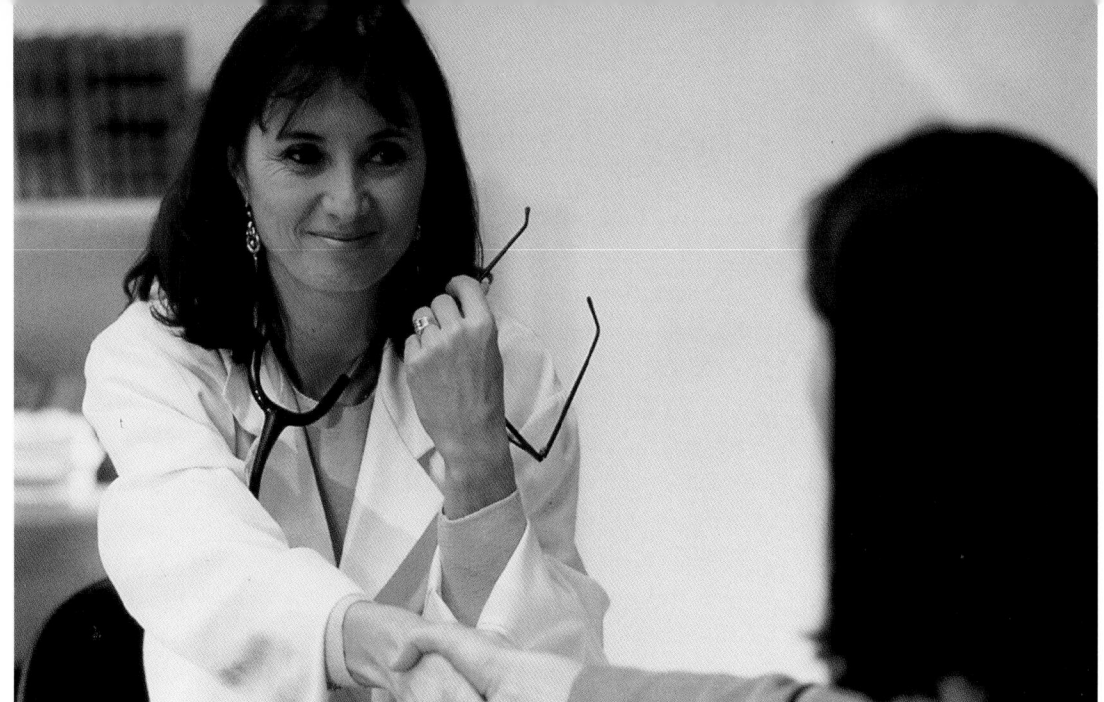

NSAIDS

NSAIDs, or non steroidal anti-inflammatory drugs, are often taken by people who suffer from chronic pain due to rheumatoid arthritis. They work by inhibiting the production of prostaglandins, the chemicals that help to pass on pain signals to the brain and also inflame surrounding tissue. Because of their pain-relieving effects, they are useful for a number of types of headache, including migraine. The NSAIDs you can obtain on prescription will be similar to the ones available over the counter, such as ibuprofen, but stronger and more potent.

NSAIDs are absorbed into the bloodstream fairly rapidly, so they begin working quickly. There are side effects commonly associated with this type of drug, including nausea, vomiting, heartburn and indigestion.

WATCHPOINT

Because of the occasional risk of bleeding, NSAIDs should be avoided by people with peptic ulcers. They are not recommended for use during pregnancy or when breastfeeding, or by people who have had an allergic reaction to aspirin. They should be used with caution by those who have asthma, digestive problems, or certain heart, kidney or liver disorders.

ANTIEMETICS

These are designed to help relieve the nausea and vomiting that often accompany migraine attacks. Antiemetics are available in a variety of forms, including tablets, soluble forms and suppositories. The suppositories are very useful for people who find that nausea or vomiting prevents them from being able to keep anything down, including a tablet. For the best results they should be taken as soon as the attack starts. Some formulations are combined with an analgesic to help prevent headache pain as well as nausea and vomiting.

WATCHPOINT

Antiemetics can cause drowsiness or lethargy, and so anyone taking them should be cautious when driving or using heavy machinery. Depending on the type of antiemetic prescribed, other side effects can include a dry mouth or blurred vision.

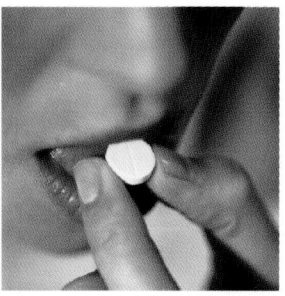

orthodox
medicines

preventative treatment

If you have frequent or severe headaches or migraines which interfere with your work and social life, your doctor may suggest that you consider a medication you take daily to help prevent the attacks, rather than something that is useful only once an attack has started. This type of drug helps break the cycle of migraine attacks, so they can be kept under control. They are not designed to be an alternative to treating an acute attack, but when a migraine does strike, it may be less severe and your usual medication may prove sufficient to keep it under control or bearable.

These drugs have not specifically been designed to treat migraine. Instead, they are more commonly used for other conditions such as high blood pressure or depression. However when taken by people with these conditions who also suffered from migraine, they were found to help keep the migraine under control.

BETA BLOCKERS

Beta blockers are commonly used to treat hypertension or high blood pressure. Their use as a treatment for migraine began in the late 1960s, when patients who were taking them for heart disorders found they also helped relieve migraine. They are thought to work because of their effects on the blood vessels. They appear to stabilize blood vessels, helping to control the process by which they open and close, and also prevent the tendency to overdilation which leads to migraine. It may also be that they have an effect on the production of serotonin, the neurochemical linked to headaches and migraine.

WATCHPOINT

The most common side effects are mild dizziness or stomach upset. If this is difficult for you to cope with discuss it with your physician. Never stop taking the medication suddenly, as this may lead to potentially serious side effects. Beta blockers are not usually suitable for people with respiratory conditions such as asthma or chronic bronchitis.

ANTIDEPRESSANTS

Antidepressants are useful for treating migraine because certain types affect the production and availability of the neurotransmitter serotonin, which is linked to the development of migraines. They can be a useful medication even if you do not suffer from depression. As with other preventative medication, it may take some weeks before the full effects of the drug are noticed.

WATCHPOINT

The side effects you may experience will vary depending on the type of antidepressant you are given. Some have a sedating effect, and can make you feel drowsy and lethargic. Others may cause effects such as a dry mouth, digestive upsets, blurred vision, dizziness, constipation or weight gain. These effects often disappear within a few days or weeks of treatment. If you experience side effects discuss this with your doctor, who may be able to find an alternative antidepressant that is equally effective in the treatment of migraine but causes you fewer problems.

None of these drugs will work immediately, so you must be willing to give the treatment time to work. Ask your doctor how long it will be before you should start to notice an improvement. If your migraines do not improve within this time, go back to see your doctor. It may be that you need a different dosage, or you may need a different treatment altogether.

RIGHT: Preventative drugs can reduce the frequency and severity of attacks, but are prescribed only in serious cases. Most take some time to make an appreciable difference.

SEROTONIN ANTAGONISTS

The most commonly used serotonin antagonist, pizotifen, works against or blocks the effects of serotonin when it is released into the body. It also appears to help raise your threshold to migraine triggers, so in effect it may take more than one trigger or a greater exposure to trigger factors before a migraine occurs.

Pizotifen comes in tablet and liquid form, and appears to be especially useful in the treatment of menstrual migraine. It is also useful for treating people who are prone to frequent and disabling migraine attacks and for whom other treatments have not proved successful. It must be taken regularly, and benefits may not be noticeable for a few months.

WATCHPOINT

The most common problem with pizotifen is that it stimulates the appetite, which leads to weight gain. Less often it may cause nausea, muscle pain, a dry mouth, dizziness or blurred vision. It is not usually suitable for use during pregnancy or breastfeeding, or by those with high blood pressure, kidney or liver disorders.

tips for taking your medicine

→ Follow the instructions carefully and take the correct dose. If the medicine is not working, do not take more than the recommended dose.

→ Ask your pharmacist if he or she can offer any special advice, such as whether you should take the tablets with meals or avoid alcohol.

→ Tell your doctor or pharmacist if you are taking any other medicines, or if you are pregnant or breastfeeding.

→ Let your doctor or pharmacist know if you suffer from any symptoms or side effects you suspect might be due to the medication. Find out if it is safe to continue taking the medicine or if you should stop immediately.

→ Carry your medication with you at all times rather than keeping it in the medicine chest. You may need it when you are out of the house.

→ Take any medication at the first sign of a headache or migraine, as this is when it will work best.

→ If your medicine does not appear to be working, see your doctor to discuss other options.

Complementary medicine has become hugely popular over the past few years, especially in the treatment of conditions associated with anxiety and stress or unhealthy lifestyle choices. There are a number of reasons for this – complementary medicine can often be used as a **self-help treatment**, the therapies are perceived to be 'natural' and therefore less harmful than orthodox medicine, and usually involve **treating the whole person** and not just the specific problem or symptom.

One of the difficulties with chronic conditions such as chronic headaches or migraines is that they can wear you down. You may feel unwell before and after an attack and so they keep you from enjoying a full and productive life. They can drain your energy levels and you can begin to see yourself as a sick person rather than someone who happens to suffer from headaches or migraines. One way to deal with this is to look for complementary therapies that, although they will not 'cure' your condition, can help you to feel better about yourself. There are a number of **complementary therapies that have been used for easing headaches and migraines very successfully**. It may take some time to find the ones that work for you, but when you do they can truly improve your overall health and well-being.

making the most of complementary medicine

In the past orthodox medical practitioners were sceptical of alternative or complementary therapies, and sadly many still are today. They often dismiss the role these therapies can play in helping patients feel better, yet more and more studies indicate that complementary therapies can be effective, particularly for stress-related conditions such as headaches and migraines. As their name implies, complementary therapies are intended to work alongside any medical treatment or drugs that you are taking. You should never stop taking any medication without discussing it with your doctor first. And you should realize that complementary therapy will not work for everyone. You may know someone whose migraine improved dramatically after acupuncture, for example, and find others who found no relief whatsoever.

It is also important to understand that complementary practitioners tailor the treatment to the individual. One person may receive one type of treatment for migraine, while another gets something completely different. This is completely normal, because the nature of treatment that people receive will vary depending on many factors including their medical history, symptoms, lifestyle and other relevant details.

choosing a therapist

At the moment, many areas of complementary health are not regulated. There are any number of organizations and bodies that provide training and qualifications for some therapies, while in other fields almost anyone can set up shop as a complementary therapist without specialist training. This is why you should take your time to find a qualified practitioner.

The best advice is to contact one of the organizations involved in the therapy. They will usually provide a list of their members practising in your area. They should also be able to explain what qualifications the practitioner will have, where or how they were trained and give a general idea of the cost of a session or treatment. They should also be able to answer questions about the therapy, and whether it would be suitable for you.

Once you have found a practitioner, find out a bit more about their qualifications, how long they have been practising and what training they have had. Do not forget to ask if they are insured to carry out this type of therapy. One of the most important aspects of your treatment is finding a therapist that you trust and feel comfortable with. They will be asking a lot of detailed questions about your medical and personal history, so you must be willing to confide in them, to establish a good working relationship, just as you would a doctor.

Many complementary therapies are not covered by private health insurance, though this will depend on the treatment, your doctor and the reason for the treatment. If you will be paying for treatment yourself, try to get some idea of how much the sessions will cost and how many you might need before you make a financial commitment. The therapist should be willing to discuss this with you.

the initial consultation

In most cases the therapist will take a detailed medical history. They will ask about your symptoms, the treatment you have already tried and how successful it has been. They will also ask about your general health and that of your family – many of the questions a medical doctor would ask.

Complementary therapists tend to look at you holistically, as a whole person, and not just at your individual symptoms. Depending on the therapist and the treatment, they may carry out blood or urine tests, take X-rays, or give you a physical examination. Once they have built up a picture of your general health, they can then put together a treatment plan that is suitable for you. The therapist may give you advice about reducing your stress levels, changing your diet or about more the personal things that are going on in your life. All these can have a bearing on your health and well-being, and may help to relieve some of your headaches and migraines.

Complementary therapy is not a quick fix; it may take time before you notice any benefit. Ask your therapist how many sessions you might need, what side effects you might encounter, and how long it should be before you notice any improvement. If you do not notice any benefit within the recommended time, it could be that this therapy is not for you.

play it safe

→ **Let your doctor know you are planning to see a complementary therapist. Ask if you can be referred to a qualified practitioner.**

→ **Contact the governing body or relevant organisation of your chosen therapy and ask for information about the treatment and a list of registered practitioners in your area.**

→ **When you have chosen a therapist, find out about their training and qualifications. Ask if they are insured to carry out the treatment you want.**

→ **Remember that complementary medicine will not be useful for every person and every complaint. Ask your therapist to be specific about what their treatment can and cannot do.**

→ **Avoid practitioners who claim to be able to cure your illness, or suggest that their treatment is suitable for almost every ailment.**

→ **Ask the therapist to keep your doctor informed of the progress of the treatment. No responsible practitioner would tell you to stop taking medication without your doctor's approval or to give up medical treatment.**

LEFT: A complementary therapist will take a holistic approach to treating your headaches or migraines, taking stock of you as an individual, your lifestyle and even your personal relationships. It is important, therefore, to open up and put your trust in them.

herbal therapy

Herbalism is probably one of the oldest forms of medicine; it has been used in many different cultures for thousands of years and involves using herbs, and other plants and flowers, to treat and prevent mental, physical and emotional ill health. Many of the conventional medicines in everyday use are the result of synthesizing traditional herbal remedies.

The two main types of herbal medicine used today are Chinese and Western herbalism. They differ in the herbs used as well as many of their diagnostic techniques.

help from complementary therapies

CHINESE HERBALISM

Chinese herbal medicine is part of the ancient system of traditional Chinese medicine (TCM), which has been practised for over five thousand years. In conjunction with acupuncture (see page 52) herbalism forms the bulk of Chinese medical treatment.

To understand Chinese medicine you need a basic understanding of the concept of yin and yang. These are the opposites that make up the whole, and there are elements of each of them in everybody. If there is an imbalance of yin or yang, Chinese herbs can help restore balance and harmony to the mind, body and emotions. The herbs prescribed will exert a specific effect on the meridian (energy line) responsible for the imbalance. This helps to rebalance the Chi, the energy or life force.

During a consultation the practitioner will note your general appearance, including your size, shape and general demeanour. He may observe the colour of your face, and examine your tongue, including its colour, coating and condition. In TCM the tongue is thought to be a good indicator of overall health and reveals the state of the spirit. The practitioner will usually take your pulse at various points around your body and ask you a number of questions. Chinese herbalists do not treat symptoms in isolation, so they will try to find out about your general health and well-being and your lifestyle.

Once a diagnosis has been made about the cause of your headaches or migraines, a prescription will be tailored to your needs. The practitioner will usually mix together a selection of the chosen herbs, and provide instructions on how to take them – they are generally boiled with water to make a tea. Some herbalists dispense the herbs on the spot, while occasionally you may need to obtain the herbs through a Chinese herbal pharmacist. In most cases you will need to go back for at least one more appointment fairly soon, so the herbalist can decide whether you are improving or whether the prescription needs adjusting.

Most herbs are safe, but you should always tell the practitioner if you have any underlying health problem, if you are pregnant or breastfeeding, or if you are taking other medicines. If you feel unwell you should stop taking the remedy immediately and contact your practitioner.

LEFT: In traditional Chinese medicine, the practitioner will play close attention to the condition of your tongue because it is believed to reveal the state of your general health.

feverfew

Various studies have shown that the herb feverfew can help to reduce the frequency and severity of migraine attacks. It also seems to help with other symptoms of migraine, such as nausea or vomiting, and to help people who suffer from chronic headaches for no obvious reason.

Feverfew is thought to work through a natural chemical it contains called parthenolide. This inhibits the release of the neurochemical serotonin, which appears to play a role in causing headaches and migraines.

Feverfew is designed as a preventive medicine and is taken over a period of time to help lessen attacks – it is not for use during a headache or migraine. Most people say it takes at least six weeks before they notice any benefits. A three-month course of feverfew could help reduce migraines for a long period of time. The easiest way to take it is in tablets or capsules. Make sure the brand you choose contains at least 0.2 per cent of the active ingredient parthenolide. Feverfew can cause side effects, including mouth ulcers, stomach pain and swollen lips. It should not be taken during pregnancy or breastfeeding.

WESTERN HERBALISM

Like Chinese herbalism, Western herbal medicine has been in use since ancient times. It uses plants as medicines to restore and maintain health by keeping the body balanced, relying on the curative qualities of plants, flowers, trees and herbs to stimulate the body's own healing system.

Herbal medicine is used to help marshal the vital force, which works to maintain our complete health, physically, mentally and emotionally. Sometimes the vital force is weakened by factors such as stress, diet and pollution, and herbalists see symptoms of disease as the result of the vital force's attempt to maintain harmony in the body.

Unlike Chinese herbs, Western herbs can be used in many different ways. They can be taken internally, as tablets or capsules, or in the form of teas, decoctions or tinctures; or used externally in creams, lotions and ointments.

A Western herbalist will ask you a number of questions to build up a picture of your health and lifestyle. They may note the condition of your skin and hair, your facial expression and how you move. They are qualified to carry out a physical examination, and so may check your pulse, take your blood pressure, test your reflexes and listen to your heart and chest.

In the case of headaches or migraines most remedies will be taken internally, in the form of a tea or tablet. Acute or short-term problems can usually be resolved within a few days and you may only need one or two appointments.

RIGHT: Western herbal medicine makes use of the healing properties of plants, such as lavender, to restore a person's life energy levels and activate his or her own healing system.

Chronic conditions may require several appointments, which allow the herbalist to check on your progress and possibly adjust your prescription as your condition improves.

Most herbs are safe when taken as recommended, but some are toxic in large doses, while others are unsuitable for use during pregnancy or breastfeeding. If you are taking herbal medicine in conjunction with conventional medicine, tell both your doctor and your therapist.

eastern therapies

These are based on the concept of the meridians and Chi, the energy or life force, which the Chinese believe drives all the cells in the body and helps to support, nourish and defend the whole person against mental, physical and emotional disease.

The Chinese believe that there are 12 main meridians, 6 of which are yin and 6 which are yang, among many other minor ones. These meridians form a network of energy channels throughout the body. Dotted along these meridians are the main acupuncture or pressure points. Stimulating these points, using needles, finger or body pressure, helps to unblock stagnant or weakened energy flow and counteract any imbalances in the body that are leading to ill health. This helps rebalance the body's energy system and restore health or prevent the development of disease.

help from complementary therapies

ACUPUNCTURE

Acupuncture makes up a major part of traditional Chinese medicine. The term literally means 'needle piercing', and involves inserting needles into the skin to stimulate specific points on the body's meridians. This stimulation helps to balance the movement of energy and increase the flow of Chi, the vital life force. Any number of ailments are said to occur when there is an imbalance or blockage of energy along these meridians. The aim of acupuncture is to help unblock them and rebalance your own personal energy flow.

Even though a number of studies have been carried out to try to discover how and why acupuncture seems to work, there are no firm answers as yet. In general, the Western view of acupuncture is that in some way it helps release endorphins, the body's natural painkillers. This is why it seems to be so successful at helping to control pain, including headaches and migraines.

During the first session the therapist will ask you questions and observe, listen, smell and touch to help reach a diagnosis. He or she may look at your tongue and eyes and take your pulses, and ask about yourself and your health. Once the therapist has decided on a course of treatment, you will need to undress sufficiently to allow access to the relevant points on the body.

The needles used during acupuncture are extremely fine, and they are usually either disposable or sterilised so you are at no risk of infection. The needles do not cause pain, though many people who have had treatment say they feel a slight tingling or numbness, and a slight ache afterwards. The usual number of needles used is between four and eight, though this can vary. The therapist will manipulate the needle to stimulate or calm the pressure point. The needles may be left in for a few minutes or up to half-an-hour.

After treatment you may feel energetic and revitalised, or you may feel a little disorientated. The number of appointments you will need depends on the problem and your overall health, but normally you should see some improvement after three or four sessions. Acupuncture works best as a preventative treatment, for conditions such as chronic headaches or migraines, rather than for relieving pain during an attack. It helps with stress-related conditions, which can affect the course of your headaches.

LEFT: In acupuncture, extremely fine needles are inserted at specific points on the body's energy pathways to improve and rebalance the energy flow. It can be very successful in treating headaches and migraines.

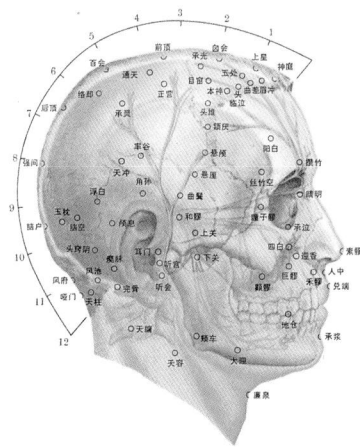

ABOVE: This traditional Chinese acupuncture chart illustrates the positioning of the acupuncture points on the right side of the head and skull.

what is acupressure?

Acupressure is similar to shiatsu in that it involves the use of finger pressure on specific acupuncture points throughout the body. This helps to stimulate the flow of Chi through the body's energy channels, or meridians.

Acupressure differs from shiatsu in that it mostly involves thumb and fingertip pressure, although it can also incorporate massage along the meridians. In the West the use of acupressure has largely been overshadowed by shiatsu. Today it is most often incorporated into other therapies such as shiatsu, or used for self-help.

SHIATSU

This originated in Japan as a holistic therapy for treating the mind, body and spirit. Although the term shiatsu means finger pressure in Japanese, this is slightly misleading, as a shiatsu practitioner will use their fingers, palms, elbows, arms, knees and feet to apply pressure to the points called 'tsubo'. These are dotted along the body's 12 main energy channels or meridians.

Shiatsu is often called 'acupuncture without needles'; this is a reasonably accurate description as both therapies share similar philosophy, principles, diagnostic methods and treatment points. The therapy is a combination of massage, pressure on acupuncture points and some manipulation. Shiatsu is said to help stimulate circulation and the flow of lymphatic tissue. This helps to release the toxins and waste products that have built up in the muscles, easing tension and encouraging relaxation.

During the treatment you are fully clothed, though you may be asked to wear loose, comfortable clothing and take off your shoes. The practitioner will ask you a number of questions about your health and well-being. He or she may also study your appearance, taking note of your shape and size, and the condition of your skin and hair.

Once the therapist has determined the root of the problem, he or she will use the fingers, thumbs, elbows and even feet to apply pressure on the specific points.

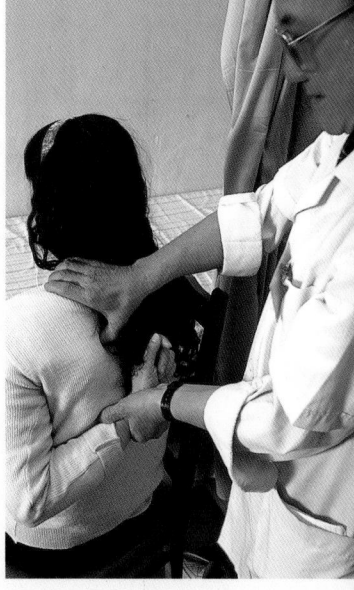

RIGHT: Shiatsu employs a combination of massage, manipulation and pressure applied to acupuncture points along the body's 12 meridians (energy channels).

This pressure is designed to release blocked energy from the meridians. In shiatsu the energy is called 'ki', the Japanese word for Chi. A session lasts about 40 minutes, and you may feel very calm and relaxed afterwards. Depending on the problem, you may need between four and eight sessions to clear up common complaints. Shiatsu is useful for stress-related conditions as well as muscle tension, both common triggers for headaches and migraines.

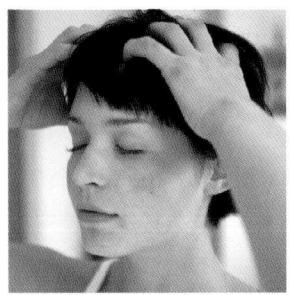

manipulation
and massage

Headaches and migraines are often caused by physical tension around the neck, shoulders and the back. For this reason the various manipulative and massage techniques can help by relieving tension. They can be used during an attack and also as a preventative measure.

help from
complementary
therapies

CHIROPRACTIC

This is a therapy that works on the musculo-skeletal system of the body, focusing mainly on the spine and its effects on the nervous system. It deals with the bones, joints, muscles, ligaments and tendons that give the body its form. By using a series of special examination and manipulative techniques, chiropractors can diagnose and treat many disorders. It is similar to osteopathy, but concentrates on specific adjustments and the manipulation of one joint at a time. Chiropractors also use X-rays as part of their diagnosis more frequently than osteopaths. Chiropractic can help with structural and non-structural illness by removing pressure from the nervous system.

Chiropractic is based on the fact that the body is a machine with a mechanical structure. If this structure, especially the spine, gets damaged, distorted or irritated the result can be acute or nagging pain. This pain can be anywhere, not just in the back or neck.

Chiropractors are trained to look for spinal nerve stress. Once this has been identified, the therapist can manipulate that particular area to correct the condition and relieve the stress so the body can restore itself back to normal. A number of studies have shown that chiropractic treatment is useful for certain types of headaches, including migraine, if they are caused by tension, stress or a misalignment of the spine.

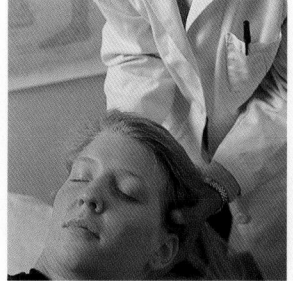

LEFT: Chiropractors concentrate on the spine and its effects on the nervous system to treat migraine and other complaints. Treatment involves manipulation of the affected areas to relieve nerve stress and allow the body to restore itself.

First, the therapist will study your spine and skeletal system, often manipulating it, and ask you to bend and move so he or she can observe your body. Once the problem has been assessed, treatment usually involves soft tissue work and manipulation, but each treatment is tailored to the individual. You may need only a couple of treatments or you may require many over a period of time. Once the problem is under control, the therapist may offer advice on posture and diet and suggest exercises to do at home.

After each session you may find you feel sore or even slightly worse for a day or so. Some people find they are full of energy, while others want to lie down and sleep. Chiropractic is safe when practised by a qualified practitioner. It is safe for pregnant women and children, though they will probably not be given X-rays. It is not suitable for people with damaged bones or bone disease.

reflexology

Reflexology is a relatively new addition to the complementary therapies. It is based on the practice of applying pressure to points on the feet, or occasionally the hands, to stimulate the body's healing system. According to reflexologists, the organs and systems of the body are reflected in specific areas on the feet, similar to the principle of meridians running through the entire body. By pressing and massaging certain areas on the soles and toes, blocked energy is released and the body's ability to heal itself is restored. Reflexology is claimed to help stress-related conditions, including headaches and migraines. During the initial consultation you will be asked questions about your health and lifestyle. Once the therapist has determined the root of the problem, he or she will use hands and thumbs to apply pressure to various parts of your feet to relieve any blockages. You should feel relaxed after treatment, though some people find their feet are a little sore. You may need a couple of treatments to relieve minor problems, but it may take more for chronic or severe conditions.

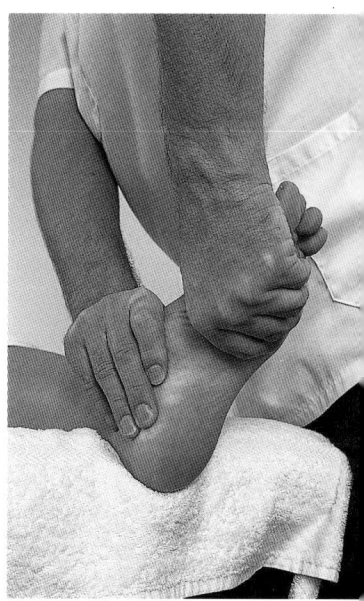

OSTEOPATHY

Osteopathy is a manipulative therapy that deals with the structural and mechanical problems in the body and is similar to chiropractic. It works on the structure – the skeleton, muscles, ligaments and connective tissue – to relieve pain, improve mobility and effectively restore all-round health.

Osteopaths believe that we function as a complete system and that our structure, organs and emotions are inter-related. So problems that affect the structure of the body also upset its balance. By manipulating the body, the osteopaths' aim is to restore health in the whole person. The focus is on easing muscular tension, as both mental and physical stress cause muscles to contract, impede circulation and lead to headaches. Many osteopaths find patients who get frequent headaches or migraines also suffer from stiffness in the neck and shoulders, or that they may have problems with or a misalignment of the upper part of the spine or the cranial (skull) bones.

The osteopath will take a detailed history, and may also use X-rays. He or she may use palpation, movement and joint testing to determine the problem. Treatment may be manipulation, soft tissue massage and high velocity thrusts to ease tense muscles. The number of sessions depends on the symptoms, but three to five can help with headaches and migraines. It is safe when practised by a qualified therapist, and can be used during pregnancy and on children.

MASSAGE

Massage is the manipulation of the body's soft tissues to promote or restore health. Massage therapists use their hands to detect and treat problems in the muscles, ligaments and tendons. There are many different types of massage, and the one chosen will depend on the specific problem. Massage can also be useful as a self-help treatment. It is useful for headaches and migraines to relieve stress and tension around the head and neck.

Massage is a very safe therapy, though you should let the therapist know if you suffer from any physical ailments such as circulatory problems, varicose veins, back disorders or are pregnant. The benefit will usually be apparent after just one treatment, as massage also helps to calm and relax. You can have a massage as often as you like, though some intense forms may leave you feeling a little sore for a couple of days so it is best not to have one every day.

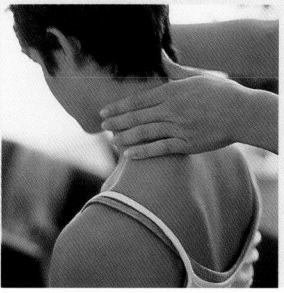

LEFT: Massage is a safe and enjoyable therapy that can relieve headaches by reducing muscle tension around the head and neck.

natural therapies

Many people like natural therapies because they feel they are safe, since they tend to use 'natural' ingredients, often made from plants, trees and flowers. They are frequently used on a self-help basis.

help from complementary therapies

AROMATHERAPY

Aromatherapy means treatment using scents, using essential oils in holistic treatments to improve health and emotional well-being. Essential oils are aromatic essences which have been distilled from flowers, trees, fruit, bark, grasses and seeds with distinctive therapeutic properties. It is thought that the chemical components in essential oils can exert specific effects on the mind and body.

The oils can be used in a number of ways, though the most common is by inhalation or by absorption through the skin, for instance during a massage or in a hot bath. It is thought that the absorption method is more effective than inhalation, because the heat of the body or hot water helps the oils be assimilated more efficiently.

You can buy essential oils from any number of outlets, such as health food shops, but you must use them carefully as some of them are quite powerful. Some oils are not suitable if you are pregnant or breastfeeding or if you have other medical conditions as well as headaches or migraines, such as high blood pressure or epilepsy. You should visit a qualified aromatherapist, who will help you decide which oils or combination of oils will be most suitable for you, discuss your condition with you, and offer practical support and advice.

HOMOEOPATHY

Homoeopathy is based on the principle that 'like is cured by like'. In practice, this means a substance that causes symptoms of illness in a healthy person can also cure the symptoms when they result from illness or disease.

BELOW: Many remedies are available over the counter.

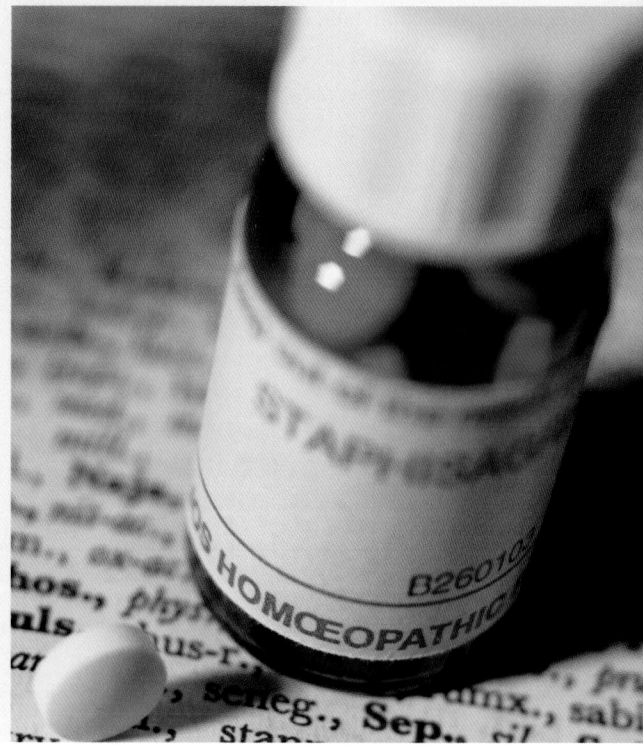

oils for headaches and migraines

Lavender oil is one of the most commonly used essential oils and is good for easing headaches and migraines. Try sprinkling a few drops on a tissue and inhale them at regular intervals. You can also rub a few drops on your temples, taking care not to get the oil near your eyes. If you suffer from nausea during a migraine attack, you may find that using ginger or peppermint oil can reduce this tendency as they help aid digestion.

RIGHT: Essential oils, distilled from plants with curative properties, are used in aromatherapy to improve both emotional and physical well-being. They are usually either inhaled or absorbed through the skin in massage or in a hot bath.

The substances that are used in treatment are known as homoeopathic remedies. These are prescribed for the individual and their reaction to the ailment, not just for the disease alone. There are over 2,000 homoeopathic remedies. The active ingredients in these remedies have been diluted many times, which is why they are safe for a wide variety of people, including children, the elderly and pregnant women.

Homoeopathy, like many other complementary therapies, does not try to suppress or treat symptoms. Practitioners see symptoms as an expression of the body's attempts to heal itself, and a positive sign that the body is fighting illness and so they should not be suppressed. The remedies are aimed at stimulating and supporting the body's healing mechanism. For this reason they can sometimes provoke what homoeopaths call an 'aggravation', whereby symptoms become worse before they get better.

During a consultation the homoeopath will begin by 'taking your case', asking numerous questions about your health, personality and lifestyle. This helps them to build up a complete picture of the type of person you are and so prescribe the best remedy. You can buy homoeopathic remedies for common ailments that are suitable for use at home.

BACH FLOWER REMEDIES

These are 38 tinctures created by Dr Edward Bach, a bacteriologist and former Harley Street doctor, who believed in treating people and not just their illnesses. He developed these remedies after he became interested in homoeopathy, believing that the dew resting on plants and flowers absorbed some of the plants' properties. Through a process of trial and error, he arrived at the present 38 remedies, designed to help every conceivable type of personality, attitude and negative state of mind.

Bach Flower Remedies are said to work because they provide the stimulus needed to kick start your own healing processes. Choosing the right remedy can prove difficult, as it very much depends on the individual's basic or true nature. You should ask a friend to help you choose a remedy or consult a therapist who uses them.

Bach Flower Remedies are most often used for mental and emotional problems rather than physical ailments. But treating the underlying emotional condition can help with any physical manifestations. Bach Flower Remedies are a self-help treatment used at home. They are safe for children as well as during pregnancy and breastfeeding.

relaxation and visualization

help from complementary therapies

Eastern philosophers and holistic medical practitioners have long believed that the mind and body function as a complete working unit, and it is now generally accepted that if the body is relaxed the mind will follow suit, and that a relaxed mind produces significant physical benefits.

Relaxation can slow down the heart rate, lower blood pressure and help to regulate breathing and the metabolic rate. It also reduces adrenaline levels, the hormones that are produced during stress, and allows the immune system to function more efficiently. By helping to reduce the effects of stress it can help treat stress-related conditions such as headaches and migraines.

RELAXATION TECHNIQUES

Relaxation techniques combat stress by providing physical and mental relief. Tension, fear and anxiety are released and replaced by feelings of calm and peace. Though stress is a normal part of everyday life, too much stress can cause physical and emotional problems.

Initially many people may find it difficult to relax, especially if they have been under a lot of stress for some time. However, once the techniques are correctly learnt, they can be performed easily and it is possible to achieve a state of relaxation and release the build-up of stress almost wherever you are and whatever you are doing.

One easy technique is the Tense Release. Tensing and releasing the muscles forms the basis of many relaxation techniques; it has been used for years and is one of the most common methods practised. The object is to tense your muscles and then release them, feeling the physical and mental release that accompanies each movement.

The best way to do this is to lie in a comfortable position with your eyes closed. Starting at the feet, tense and hold each of the major muscle groups for ten seconds while you breathe calmly and deeply, then release the muscles. Continue tensing and releasing all other muscle groups, such as the legs, the arms, the neck and shoulders. After about 10 to 20 minutes open your eyes, stretch your body and see how relaxed and refreshed you feel.

VISUALIZATION

Visualization, often called creative imagery, uses your mind to conjure up images that make you feel relaxed. By using the imagination to create attractive and positive images, you can heal or change aspects of your life. Visualization is used both for improving physical ailments and conditions, and also for making positive improvements to destructive attitudes or behaviour. It is often used in conjunction with relaxation techniques. Again, it is easy to learn and can be done almost anywhere and at any time.

> **Find a place where you can sit or lie without interruption. Close your eyes and start to breathe slowly and deeply.**
> **Try to clear your mind of your worries or other problems.**
> **Retreat in your mind to a place that has a special, positive significance. Imagine a peaceful place in which you are safe, calm and relaxed, such as the mountains or by the sea. Choose any place that works for you and helps you to relax.**
> **Draw a clear image in your mind of exactly what it would be like to be in this peaceful place. Use all of your senses to explore this place. Imagine how it looks, sounds and smells. Continue with your measured breathing.**
> **As the picture becomes more real, you will find yourself relaxing and you will become less tense and stressed.**
> **You can stay in this place for as long as you wish. When you feel relaxed, slowly bring yourself back to the present. Imagine yourself leaving your peaceful place and coming back to everyday life. Slowly open your eyes and stand or sit up gently. You should now feel relaxed and refreshed.**

meditation

Meditation is a relaxation technique that frees the mind from distressing thoughts. It is similar to the self-help relaxation techniques, but often involves focusing on a repetitive sound, word or image to empty the mind. .

There are a number of different schools of meditation and probably the best known is Transcendental Meditation. There have been a number of clinical trials which seem to confirm that this therapy can help relieve stress, lower blood pressure, reduce headaches and migraines and ease other stress-related problems. Many people report feeling peaceful, calm and relaxed after meditation and these benefits can last for quite a while.

Although you do not need to see a practitioner to learn to meditate, it is best to be taught by experts to ensure you are using the techniques correctly and getting the most benefit. With Transcendental Meditation, it is recommended that you meditate for 20 minutes twice a day. With other types, you only have to use them when you feel the need.

ABOVE: Meditation can be a useful therapy in the relief of headaches and migraines. It works by reducing stress levels and helping to relax the mind and body.

quick relaxation trick

This technique can be used at any time you feel stress building up. You can do it as often as you feel the need. As you begin to feel better, you may find that performing the technique a few times a week is sufficient.

→ Find a quiet place where you won't be disturbed. Sit or lie in a comfortable position.
→ Close your eyes and make yourself aware of your body. Avoid thinking about your problems. Instead, concentrate on the areas of your body where you notice muscle tension. Make an effort to relax those areas, such as the shoulders and neck.
→ Pay attention to your breathing. Breathe deeply through your nose, focusing on each breath. Relax your mouth and jaw, letting your tongue fall away from the roof of your mouth.
→ Allow your breathing to become deeper, longer and slower, and extend your inhaling and exhaling. Make sure you are breathing deep in the abdomen. When your mind wanders, which is natural, bring it back to concentrate on your breathing.
→ After about five minutes, gently begin to stir your body. Open your eyes, and sit or stand slowly and carefully. You should feel relaxed and refreshed.

movement therapies

Physical tension is known to be one of the triggers of both headaches and migraines, particularly when it affects the neck and shoulders. This tension can be the result of poor posture, emotional anxiety or stress. Learning to use your body correctly and keeping it mobile and supple may provide some relief from your symptoms.

help from
complementary
therapies

ALEXANDER TECHNIQUE

The Alexander Technique was developed by Frederick Matthias Alexander, who believed that misuse of the body, which is often exhibited by poor posture and movement, can lead to tension. He developed techniques which are a combination of verbal instructions and manual guidance to help people learn to use their bodies correctly.

The Alexander Technique is not a therapy as such, but a process of re-education which aims to teach us to rediscover our natural poise, grace and freedom and use our bodies more efficiently. It is often referred to as posture training, which is not strictly correct, although improved postural balance is often an obvious benefit. The Alexander Technique is taught in classes. It is not used to alleviate specific ailments, but to address the source of them. It has been found that in the process of restoring harmony to the whole person, specific problems often disappear.

Lessons take place on a one-to-one basis and begin with a discussion between you and your teacher about why you have come and what help you hope to get from the course. If you have a particular problem, ask if the Alexander Technique can help. Wear loose, comfortable clothing, though you do not need to remove any clothes during a lesson except possibly your shoes.

During the lesson you may be asked to carry out movements, such as walking, bending, sitting and lifting to see how your body works. The teacher will guide and direct you in all these activities so that you can feel how effortless and smooth the movement can be. Throughout the lesson the teacher will talk to you about what he or she is doing, pointing out your bad habits and teaching you how to replace them with good ones.

You may be given 'homework' to practice regularly, including breathing exercises. Usually, about 30 lessons are required, though there are no hard and fast rules.

LEFT: The Alexander Technique re-educates the body to move correctly and efficiently, in order to relieve tension built up through unconsciously acquiring bad physical habits, such as poor posture.

RIGHT: Yoga involves both breathing techniques, to help relax the mind and body, and exercise postures, to tone the muscles, improve circulation and flush toxins from the body.

YOGA

Yoga has been practised for over 3,000 years, the word 'yoga' coming from the Sanskrit word for union. Practising the discipline is believed to encourage the union of mind, body and spirit and restore the whole person to balance.

It is a gentle exercise system that benefits both body and spirit. It involves a combination of exercise postures, called 'asanas', and breathing techniques known as 'pranayamas', as well as 'dhyanas', or meditation techniques. The breathing techniques are essential for relaxation and meditation, while the postures exercise the body muscles and also help encourage relaxation. The postures are performed in a particular sequence designed to exercise all the major muscle groups in the correct order. This encourages good circulation and helps flush toxins out of the body. By combining these techniques yoga has been shown to help with relaxation and stress reduction. Yoga benefits the body by relaxing muscles and improving suppleness, fitness and physical function.

Yoga is usually taught in classes of up to 20 people, lasting from one to two hours, but you may also find much smaller classes or even one-to-one sessions. It is performed barefoot, and it is best to wear loose and comfortable clothing to allow you free range of movement. Tell the teacher if you are suffering from any physical illnesses or disabilities, so he or she can advise you on which movements to avoid or adapt. Drink plenty of fluids before a yoga class and avoid eating a heavy meal within two hours of it.

For it to have a lasting effect yoga should be practised regularly. Once you have learnt the movements you can practice at home. Yoga is safe and can be practised by children, the elderly, pregnant women and by people with chronic health problems. Many headache and migraine sufferers have taken up yoga and found that it helps, especially for relaxation. Yoga is also an excellent exercise and helps to improve strength and flexibility as well as reducing physical tension in the upper body, the trigger for many headaches and migraines.

One of the most important things you can do to help yourself is to **pay attention to your diet and eating habits**. As you may know from your own experience, these are often responsible for triggering headaches and migraine. Serotonin, the neurochemical which appears to play a major part in migraine attacks, can be released by consuming certain foods and drinks, and **headaches are said to be a common symptom of food intolerance or allergy**. Low blood sugar can also trigger an attack, so the number and content of your meals can play an important role.

The good news is that, unlike trigger factors such as changes in the weather over which you have no control, you can do something about what and how you eat. In this chapter, you'll find the information and advice you need to take charge of your diet and eating habits. It explains in detail the role foods and drinks play and examines the various reasons why **certain food and drink may bring on a headache**.

Most important of all, it gives **advice on how you can modify your diet and eating habits** to help reduce the number of your headaches or migraines, and even the severity of your attacks.

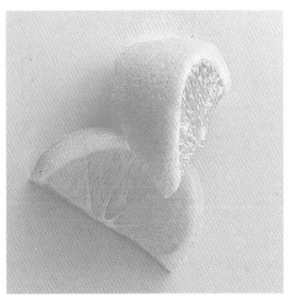

common dietary triggers

→ **Tea, coffee and other caffeinated drinks such as colas, cocoa and chocolate. Painkillers containing caffeine may also be a trigger**

→ **Alcohol, especially red wine, brandy, whisky and sherry**

→ **Chocolate, especially dark chocolate**

→ **Peanuts**

→ **Yeast extract and yeast products**

→ **Processed and smoked meats such as bacon, salami, pepperoni, frankfurters, chipolatas, chorizo, corned beef and mortadella**

→ **Citrus fruits such as oranges, lemons, grapefruit, citrus fruit juices and marmalade**

→ **Bananas**

→ **Onions**

→ **Smoked fish such as smoked haddock, kippers and mackerel**

→ **Shellfish**

→ **Chicken livers**

→ **Pickles and pickled foods like sauerkraut and olives**

→ **Sourdough bread**

→ **Wheat and wheat products such as bread, cereals and pasta**

→ **Broad beans, lentils, peas and mangetout**

→ **Dairy products such as milk and cheese**

→ **Figs, dates and raisins**

→ **Red-skinned fruits such as red plums and raspberries**

In common with the many triggers mentioned in Chapter 2, the things you eat and drink can vary in their effects. Many foods and drinks will trigger a headache soon after consumption. Others may be eaten as long as 36 hours before a headache strikes. This is because it takes time for the offending chemical to be digested and enter the liver. However, this can be confusing if you are trying to pinpoint your various trigger factors.

Keeping a trigger diary will help you trace the foods that are particular culprits in your headaches or migraines. You may well find that you can eat some trigger foods in small quantities without any problems, but that if you eat more you get a headache.

The amount needed to trigger a headache or migraine varies from person to person. This is known as your trigger threshold. For example, you may be able to get away with eating one slice of pepperoni pizza but two slices push you over your threshold and set off a migraine attack. Thus two slices is your trigger threshold. Knowing your trigger threshold can help you to plan your diet, so you do not always have to forgo things that you enjoy.

There are a number of foods and drinks that are well-recognized headache and migraine triggers. The most common offenders are foods and drinks containing caffeine, chocolate, preserved meats, fermented foods and alcohol. However there are many others (see left) and there may be a few which do not trigger a headache or migraine in other people but which do in you. You will need to do some detective work to help you identify which ones most affect you.

chemical reactions

VASOACTIVE AMINES

Many of the foods that trigger headaches or migraines contain a group of natural chemicals known as vasoactive amines. These substances act on the blood vessels, causing them to widen or narrow. It is this change in the size of the blood vessels that triggers the cycle of pain.

Vasoactive amines are usually highest in foods that have decomposed or fermented during processing. Amines are absorbed more readily in the presence of fat, one reason why high-fat amine-containing foods like cheese and chocolate can be so problematic for migraine sufferers. It is thought that people who get migraines may be short of the enzyme monoamine oxidase, which breaks down amines during digestion.

There are various types of amines. One of the main ones, tyramine, is found in cheeses, especially blue and mature cheeses, like Gorgonzola, Danish blue or blue Stilton, although not in soft cream cheese and cottage cheeses, which may not cause problems. Tyramine is also found in red wine. One of the biggest culprits is the Italian wine Chianti. The skins of the grapes used to make the wine are especially high in tyramine. Changing to drinking white wine, rosé, a lighter red wine or diluting wine in a spritzer may help banish your headaches or migraines. Tyramine is also present in yeast extracts such as Marmite and Vegemite, and in Horlicks, liver, sausages, broad beans and pickled herrings.

Phenylethylamine, another amine, is found in chocolate (the darker the chocolate the more it contains). Histamine, a third amine probably best known for the part it plays in allergic reactions such as hay fever, is found in cheese, sauerkraut, salami and sausagemeat as well as in red wine and other alcoholic drinks. A fourth amine known as synephrine is found in citrus fruits, their juices and products like marmalade.

ABOVE: Many cheeses, particularly blue and mature cheeses, contain tyramine, a chemical that affects the size of blood vessels which is known to cause headaches.

NITRATES AND NITRITES

Other culprits are nitrates and nitrites, chemicals found naturally in small quantities in foods such as beetroot, celery, lettuce, spinach, radishes and rhubarb. Nitrates and nitrites are also used in processed meats such as bacon, salami, pepperoni and frankfurters, to preserve them and give them their red colour. They are converted in the stomach into other chemicals called nitrosamines.

MONOSODIUM GLUTAMATE

Another chemical which commonly causes problems is monosodium glutamate, or MSG, a salt form of an amino acid used in food preservation and flavouring. You may find it listed on food labels where it may be referred to as hydrolysed protein or E621. MSG is often an ingredient of Oriental foods and flavourings like soy sauce – causing the 'Chinese Restaurant Syndrome', which involves a headache together with perspiration and a feeling of tightness and pressure in the face and chest. MSG is also used in processed meats and canned foods. The chemical is absorbed quickly and reactions often come on within half-an-hour of eating a food that contains it.

FOOD ADDITIVES

Many of the additives used in food manufacture cause problems for headache and migraine sufferers. As well as those already described, these include artificial sweeteners, such as aspartame used as a sugar-substitute in many 'diet' foods and drinks like mousses, whips and soft drinks; tartrazine (E102) used to colour foods yellow; sulphur dioxide used in dried fruits; salt and sodium benzoate.

CAFFEINE

Caffeine is a curious case. Drinking too many caffeinated drinks such as tea, coffee and colas will frequently trigger a headache or migraine. Caffeine is also found in varying quantities in bars of chocolate. However, suddenly stopping caffeine consumption will trigger a 'caffeine-withdrawal' headache, usually within about 18 hours. This is thought to be one reason why some people get headaches only at weekends. They have a heavy caffeine intake during the week when they are working but drink much less coffee and tea at weekends.

Intriguingly, caffeine is also an ingredient in many headache remedies. This is because a small amount of caffeine enhances the action of analgesics (painkillers) such as aspirin and paracetamol. You may have noticed that if you drink a cup of tea or coffee with a painkiller it helps it to act more quickly. In addition drinking a cup of tea or coffee if you are feeling 'headachy' will often fend off a headache by acting as a mild stimulant.

If you find that caffeine is one of your triggers you may have to accept that cutting down on or giving up some of your favourite foods and drinks is the only way to become free of headaches. Only you can decide whether this is a price worth paying. Good quality coffee made with arabica beans contains less caffeine than that made from poorer quality beans, so if you are reluctant to give up your caffeine fix it may be that you can tolerate the occasional cup of a really good quality coffee. Likewise the caffeine content of strong teas such as Assam are higher than other teas. With a bit of experimenting you may still be able to enjoy a cup of tea.

Amines are contained in a wide variety of foods, and trying to avoid them may seem all but impossible. Try to eliminate the following, a food at a time, and then re-introduce them into your diet. If you are symptom-free when the food is excluded, and the symptoms reappear when it is re-introduced, it could be a source of your problem.

→ **Chocolate**
→ **Yogurt**
→ **Cheese – matured and blue**
→ **Shellfish**
→ **Game**
→ **Bananas, pineapple and raspberries**
→ **Citrus fruits, juices and marmalade**
→ **Plums**
→ **Broad beans and peas**
→ **Avocados**
→ **Yeast and meat extracts**
→ **Smoked and pickled fish**
→ **Pickled products such as sauerkraut**
→ **Red wine**
→ **Horlicks**

If amines are a problem for you (check your trigger diary) then sticking to an amine-free diet for a couple of months may bring a striking reduction in your migraines. If you then re-introduce the foods you have eliminated one by one you should be able to find if any specific ones have an effect.

However, it may be the amount of amine released overall rather than a particular food which causes you problems. You may find that you can eat small amounts of amine-containing foods but if you go overboard a migraine will strike. With time and perseverance you will learn how much or how little you can take.

eating patterns and habits

Low blood sugar levels, caused by skipping meals, irregular mealtimes or dieting, are one of the most common headache and migraine triggers. Eating little and often can help iron out dips in your blood sugar, so you should aim to eat three meals and a couple of snacks every day. Try especially to get a good breakfast, as you have been fasting for eight hours and your blood sugar levels are likely to be low. Skipping breakfast may lead to a headache later in the day.

The best foods to maintain stable blood sugar levels are known as complex carbohydrates. They include starchy foods such as baked potatoes, whole grains, such as brown rice and wholemeal bread, and vegetables, so aim to eat some of these at every meal. Low blood sugar is most likely to occur if you are hungry or after exercise. If you pay attention you may be able to recognize when your blood sugar level is becoming low – you may feel weak, shaky and slightly light-headed – and take preventive action. Try eating a slice of wholemeal toast with peanut butter, a banana or a piece of fruit. If you need to lose weight make sure you diet sensibly. Once again you should aim to eat little and often and opt for a diet based around complex carbohydrates.

Dehydration is often a factor in headaches, and few of us drink enough during the course of a day. We need about two or three litres of fluid to make up for what is lost through normal activities. While some of that comes from our food, we need to top it up with extra fluid. The best choice is water, either tap, filtered, spring or mineral. Avoid increasing your fluid intake through coffee and tea, and do not rely on sugary drinks, as these can cause fluctuations in blood sugar levels, which in turn can lead to headaches.

nutritional deficiencies

Many alternative and complementary practitioners believe that shortages of essential vitamins, minerals and other nutrients are a factor in headaches and migraines. Generally speaking we ought to be able to get all the nutrients we need from our food. However, this may be difficult to achieve. And it may be complicated by the problem of food allergy and intolerance (see below), which prevents the body from processing all the nutrients consumed. Complementary practitioners claim that supplementing your diet with these missing nutrients can help to avert headaches and migraines. The subject is complicated because it has also been found that large doses of certain vitamins may actually trigger a migraine. However, this may be because of additives used in the preparation of vitamin supplements.

Some practitioners claim that taking nutrients that prevent the red blood cells, known as platelets, from clumping together can help avert migraine. This clumping mechanism is thought to be one of the factors involved in inducing the cycle of pain in migraine (it is the platelets that release serotonin). Antiplatelet nutrients include vitamin B6, vitamin C and vitamin E.

Substances known as essential fatty acids, which the body cannot manufacture, also have an antiplatelet effect. Good sources are linseed oil and evening primrose oil. Ginger (available in capsule form from health food stores) is worth a try, as it helps dilate constricted blood vessels and has an antiplatelet effect. Some studies have found that taking a daily fish oil supplement can reduce the incidence of severe headaches. This may be a result of the antiplatelet activity of fish oils, so it may be worth trying one or more of these and seeing if they help.

Other nutrients sometimes recommended are vitamin A, folic acid, pantothenic acid, vitamins B1 and B12. The B vitamin called niacin, which helps relax the blood vessels, can be especially useful, although this can trigger a migraine attack if taken in excess. The minerals calcium and magnesium, which have a natural tranquillizing effect, may help too.

The action of vitamins and minerals is complicated and taking too much of one can lead to an imbalance in others. For this reason one of the best ways to ensure that you get the ones you require is to take a multi-vitamin and mineral supplement. If you have a problem with food intolerance check that any supplement you buy does not contain artificial flavourings, colourings, yeast (often used in the synthesis of B vitamins) or wheatgerm (used to produce vitamin E).

food allergy and intolerance

Although many conventional doctors dismiss the idea, many alternative and complementary practitioners believe that food allergy and/or intolerance are culprits in causing headaches and migraines. A number of studies have been made and while several have shown foods to be a problem, none proves conclusively that allergy or intolerance to these foods is definitely the reason for the headaches.

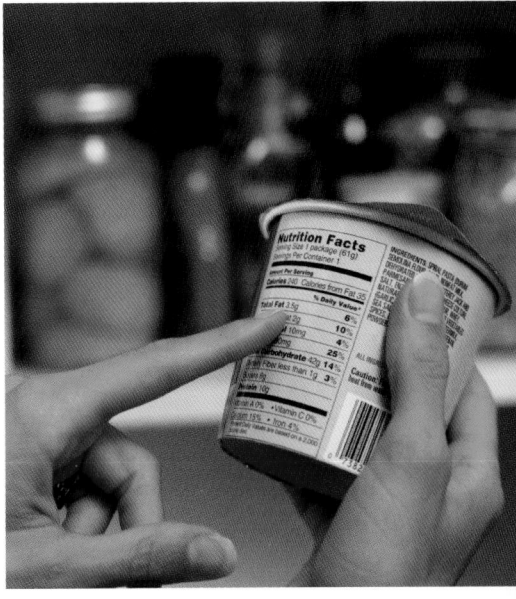

ABOVE: Keep a check on the ingredients used in your food to ensure that your diet is rich in vitamins and minerals.

BELOW: Complex carbo-hydrates such as rice will prevent your blood sugar levels dropping and plenty of water will lessen the risk of dehydration – both common causes of migraines.

the role of food
in headaches
and migraines

The terms allergy and intolerance are often used interchangeably but there are important differences. Food allergy proper is relatively rare. It is when the immune system, which exists to protect the body from invasion, reacts to a food as if it were an invader. It produces specific antibodies, histamine and other substances, to fight off the threat. Common allergy-provoking foods include milk, wheat, shellfish, eggs, nuts and fruit. Symptoms include urticaria (hives) and skin rashes, digestive problems and nasal inflammation. In extreme cases, anaphylactic shock can result, in which the tissues of the mouth and the airways swell on contact with the food leading to breathing difficulty and circulatory failure.

Food intolerance, or food sensitivity, is much more common than food allergy. It is an unpleasant reaction to food that does not involve an immune response. Unlike allergy, where there is a particular immune response, there are thought to be several reasons why food intolerance occurs. Some people are short of certain enzymes necessary for the proper digestion of certain foods. For example, deficiency of the enzyme lactase makes it difficult for those affected to digest milk – another reason why dairy products may trigger a headache or migraine. An inability to digest gluten, a protein found in wheat flour, may also cause problems for some people.

Some experts have also found that people who are prone to migraines metabolize the mineral copper differently to other people. Foods containing copper include our old friends chocolate, shellfish, nuts and wheatgerm, while citrus fruits like oranges and lemons cause more copper to be absorbed, which could be why orange juice and marmalade often trigger migraines.

Other mechanisms in food sensitivity may be the effects of chemicals in food, such as caffeine, amines or artificial additives such as the food colouring tartrazine or the artificial sweetener aspartame. Other foods such as shellfish cause the body to release histamine, a body chemical that causes the blood vessels to dilate.

In the light of this it is hardly surprising that a wide number of foods can cause symptoms of intolerance, including those that can cause food allergies. However the main offenders are wheat, rye, oats, corn, milk and milk produce, beef, eggs, chicken, chocolate, tea and coffee, food colourings and preservatives, yeast, pork, peanuts, citrus fruits and alcohol. Those least likely to cause problems include lamb, turkey, pears, Brussels sprouts, courgettes, cauliflower, carrots and broccoli.

detecting food allergy and intolerance

There are a wide range of symptoms attributed to food allergies and intolerance. As well as headaches and migraines, they include muscle and joint aches and pains, digestive upsets such as bloating, constipation

BELOW: Eggs, milk and other dairy products are common allergy-provoking foods.

and diarrhoea, fatigue, skin disorders such as eczema, low blood sugar, sweating and flushing, weight gain and fluid retention. Some allergy specialists attribute emotional and mental problems such as depression, anxiety and hyperactivity to food allergy.

The main way to discover whether food allergy or intolerance is contributing to your headaches and migraine is known as the exclusion diet. In broad terms it involves eliminating a suspect food or substance from your diet and then re-introducing it to see whether it provokes a headache or migraine. It is also worth noting if you are symptom-free during the exclusion period.

Although it is possible to put yourself on an exclusion diet, it is probably best done under the supervision of a doctor, dietician or nutritional therapist. They are able to develop a safe exclusion diet and also interpret the results more accurately. Children should never be put on an exclusion diet without medical advice.

If you do decide to go it alone you need to realize that it is a time-consuming process. Each food must be excluded for up to three weeks before you will be able to determine if it is causing you problems. And if a number of foods are suspect, it can take quite a while to check them all. For this reason it will be much easier if you pick a time when you will be able to stick to the diet. Avoid times such as Christmas or holidays, and start when you are least likely to be disrupted by withdrawal symptoms, for example over the weekend. Initially you may suffer withdrawal headaches, migraines and cravings in the first three to five days of leaving out the suspect food. However, if you are intolerant of the food, you should begin to feel better after this period.

After three weeks of exclusion introduce a normal-sized portion of the food into your diet and see if you get a headache or migraine. You need to allow up to 36 hours before deciding that there has not been an adverse reaction, as a migraine can take this long to develop. If a reaction does occur, stop eating the offending food and wait for the headache or migraine to ease before re-introducing another food. Three weeks is the maximum time you should wait before re-introducing a food. If it is excluded for longer its re-introduction may not result in symptoms, leading to the erroneous conclusion that the offending food is not responsible for your headaches or migraines.

Once you have identified the food or foods that cause you problems you can eliminate them from your diet. If you do leave foods out of your diet it is important to substitute a nutritious alternative, otherwise you may begin to experience nutrient deficiencies. This is where the advice from a professional, a doctor, dietician or nutritional therapist, can be of such value. After six months to a year you can try the food again to see if it still causes you problems. If it does not you can re-introduce it to your diet, although it is best only to eat it occasionally and in moderation, or you may develop an intolerance to it again.

ABOVE: Chocolate can often cause symptoms of intolerance, such as headaches, but you may find that you can enjoy it in small quantities without suffering any ill effects.

chapter 6

Certain foods are thought to be triggers for some types of headaches and migraines. Exclusion diets (see page 69), in which specific foods are removed from the diet and then gradually re-introduced to see if they cause a problem, are best done under medical supervision. However, it is possible for you to experiment safely yourself. This involves scrupulously avoiding a particular food for a few weeks and then eating it again. If your symptoms return, it is possible that this food is one of your triggers.

Some foods, such as chocolate, citrus fruits and cheese, are easy to avoid. Others may be more difficult and are sometimes included in ready-made meals or canned or packaged foods that you use in a recipe. For this reason it is crucial that you read the list of ingredients of any ready-made foodstuffs carefully.

Another problem is finding enough different meals to eat over a period of time that do not include some of the potential triggers. **The recipes in this chapter are all designed to exclude common triggers**. This should make it easier for you to choose healthy recipes for yourself and your family while you are trying to find out which foods affect you.

chilli bean and pepper soup

Serves 6 – Preparation time: 20 minutes – Cooking time: 40 minutes

Per serving – Energy: 217 kcals/912 kJ · Protein: 8 g · Carbohydrate: 26 g · Fat: 16 g · Fibre: 7 g

✔	alcohol free
	citrus free
	dairy free
✔	gluten free
✔	wheat free

2	**tablespoons sunflower oil**
1	**large onion, finely chopped**
4	**garlic cloves, finely chopped**
2	**red peppers, cored, deseeded and diced**
2	**red chillies, deseeded and finely chopped**
900 ml	**(1¹/₂ pints) vegetable stock**
750 ml	**(1¹/₄ pints) tomato juice or passata**
1	**tablespoon double-concentrate tomato purée**
1	**tablespoon sun-dried tomato paste**
2	**tablespoons sweet chilli sauce, or more to taste**
400 g	**(13 oz) can red kidney beans, drained**
2	**tablespoons finely chopped fresh coriander**
	salt
	pepper
	rind of 1 lime, cut into strips, to garnish (optional)

To Serve:

75 ml	**(3 fl oz) soured cream**
	tortilla chips

1 Heat the oil in a large saucepan and fry the onion and garlic until soft but not coloured. Stir in the peppers and chillies and fry for a few minutes. Stir in the stock and tomato juice or passata, the tomato purée and paste, chilli sauce, kidney beans and coriander. Bring to the boil, cover and simmer for 30 minutes.

2 Leave to cool slightly, then purée in a food processor or blender until smooth. Return the soup to the pan, taste and adjust the seasoning if necessary. Add a little extra chilli sauce if you like. Bring to the boil and serve in warmed soup bowls. Swirl a little soured cream into each portion and serve with tortilla chips. Garnish with strips of lime rind, if liked.

fava

Serves 4 – Preparation time: 5 minutes – Cooking time: 40–45 minutes

Per serving – Energy: 170 kcals / 710 kJ · Protein: 3 g · Carbohydrate: 8 g · Fat: 14 g · Fibre: 2 g

50 g (2 oz) yellow split peas, rinsed
4 tablespoons extra virgin olive oil
1 small garlic clove, crushed
1 tablespoon lemon juice
$^1/_4$ teaspoon ground cumin
$^1/_2$ teaspoon mustard powder
pinch of cayenne pepper
salt
pepper

To Garnish:
1 tablespoon chopped parsley
pinch of cayenne pepper
1 tablespoon extra virgin olive oil

To Serve:
prepared raw vegetables
warm pitta bread

This puréed bean paste is similar to hummus, but is made with yellow split peas.

1 Put the split peas into a saucepan and add enough cold water to cover them by about 2.5 cm (1 inch). Bring to the boil and simmer over a low heat, stirring frequently, for 30–35 minutes until all the water has been absorbed and the peas are cooked. Leave to cool slightly.

2 Place the peas in a food processor or blender with all the remaining ingredients, season to taste with salt and pepper, and process until smooth. Add 2–3 tablespoons of boiling water if the mixture is too thick.

3 Transfer the purée to a serving dish and sprinkle with the parsley and cayenne pepper. Drizzle with olive oil. Serve with a selection of prepared raw vegetables and warm pitta bread for dipping.

alcohol free	✔
citrus free	
dairy free	✔
gluten free	
wheat free	

smoked haddock chowder

Serves 4 – Preparation time: 10–15 minutes – Cooking time: 30 minutes

Per serving – Energy: 268 kcals/1138 kJ · Protein: 31 g · Carbohydrate: 32 g · Fat: 3 g · Fibre: 3 g

✔	alcohol free
✔	citrus free
	dairy free
✔	gluten free
✔	wheat free

500 g	(1 lb) potatoes, cut into 1 cm (¹/₂ inch) cubes
1	onion, finely chopped
1	bay leaf
¹/₂	teaspoon chopped marjoram
600 ml	(1 pint) water
500 g	(1 lb) skinned smoked haddock fillet, chopped
¹/₄	teaspoon ground nutmeg
450 ml	(³/₄ pint) semi-skimmed milk
	white pepper
2	tablespoons finely chopped marjoram, to garnish

1 Combine the potatoes, onion, bay leaf and marjoram with the measured water in a large heavy-based saucepan. Bring the mixture to the boil, then lower the heat, cover and simmer for 5 minutes.

2 Add the chopped haddock, nutmeg and milk to the pan and season to taste with white pepper. Simmer the soup, partially covered, for 20 minutes.

3 Serve the chowder in warmed soup bowls, garnished with marjoram.

new potato salad with wholegrain mustard cream

Serves 4 – Preparation time: 8 minutes – Cooking time: 15 minutes

Per serving – Energy: 342 kcals/1427 kJ · Protein: 8 g · Carbohydrate: 32 g · Fat: 21 g · Fibre: 21 g

✔	alcohol free
✔	citrus free
	dairy free
✔	gluten free
✔	wheat free

750 g	(1¹/₂ lb) small new potatoes
50 g	(2 oz) thinly sliced Parma ham
150 ml	(¹/₄ pint) double cream
2	tablespoons wholegrain mustard
	salt
	pepper

To Garnish (optional):
flat-leaf parsley, roughly torn
chive flowers

1 Cook the potatoes in a pan of boiling water for about 15 minutes, until tender. Drain and rinse briefly in cold water to halt the cooking process. Drain again thoroughly and transfer them to a bowl to cool slightly.

2 Cook the Parma ham under a preheated hot grill for 2–2¹/₂ minutes, turning it once, until crisp and golden. Set aside.

3 In a small bowl, stir together the cream and mustard until the mixture begins to thicken. Mix the dressing with the potatoes while they are still warm, adding salt and pepper to taste.

4 Serve the salad warm or cold with the Parma ham crumbled over the top. Sprinkle with the parsley leaves and scatter with chive flowers, if liked.

mixed leaf salad with spiced toasted nuts

Serves 4 – Preparation time: 10 minutes – Cooking time: 6–10 minutes
Per serving – Energy: 352 kcals/1450 kJ · Protein: 6 g · Carbohydrate: 4 g · Fat: 35 g · Fibre: 2 g

175–250 g (6–8 oz) mixed salad leaves,
    such as lollo rosso, lamb's lettuce,
    young spinach, frisée, rocket,
    red oakleaf
small handful of chervil or dill sprigs

Spiced Nuts:

25 g   (1 oz) butter
50 g   (2 oz) blanched almonds
50 g   (2 oz) pecan nuts
  2   tablespoons pine nuts
  1   teaspoon Worcestershire sauce
  1   teaspoon mild chilli powder
    pinch of ground cumin

Vinaigrette Dressing:

  3   tablespoons olive oil
  3   tablespoons white wine vinegar
  1   teaspoon Dijon mustard
    pinch of sugar
    salt
    pepper

1 To make the spiced nuts, melt the butter in a saucepan. Add the nuts, Worcestershire sauce, chilli powder and cumin and cook over a moderate heat for 1 minute. Tip into a baking tin and place under a preheated moderate grill. Cook, turning frequently, for 5–10 minutes until the nuts are toasted. Leave to cool.

2 To make the vinaigrette dressing, mix together the olive oil, vinegar, mustard and sugar then season with salt and pepper.

3 Mix the salad leaves and herbs in a large salad bowl. Spoon the dressing over the leaves and toss to coat, then scatter the spiced nuts over the top.

alcohol free	
citrus free	✔
dairy free	
gluten free	✔
wheat free	✔

roasted asparagus with coriander and lime

Serves 4 – Preparation time: 10 minutes – Cooking time: about 20 minutes

Per serving – Energy: 246 kcals/1010 kJ · Protein: 6 g · Carbohydrate: 4 g · Fat: 23 g · Fibre: 3 g

✔	alcohol free
	citrus free
✔	dairy free
✔	gluten free
✔	wheat free

750 g **(1¹/₂ lb) asparagus spears**
8 **tablespoons olive oil**
3 **tablespoons freshly squeezed lime juice**
coarse sea salt
pepper

To Garnish:
torn coriander leaves
lime wedges

1 Trim the asparagus and arrange it in a single layer in a shallow roasting tin.

2 Spoon 4 tablespoons of the olive oil over the asparagus and shake lightly to mix. Roast in a preheated oven at 200°C (400°F), Gas Mark 6 for about 20 minutes until just tender, turning the asparagus once during cooking. Leave to cool.

3 Transfer the roasted asparagus spears to a shallow dish. Spoon the remaining olive oil and the lime juice over the top. Sprinkle with the salt and pepper and toss lightly. Garnish with coriander and lime wedges and serve.

hot chicken liver salad

Serves 4 – Preparation time: 20 minutes – Cooking time: 3–4 minutes

Per serving – Energy: 298 kcals/1235 kJ · Protein: 23 g · Carbohydrate: 1 g · Fat: 22 g · Fibre: 1 g

25 g	**(1 oz) butter**
5	**tablespoons light olive oil**
500 g	**(1 lb) chicken livers, halved**
2	**tablespoons red wine vinegar**
1	**teaspoon wholegrain mustard**
250 g	**(8 oz) mixed salad leaves,**
	such as red oakleaf, frisée,
	radicchio, chicory
2	**spring onions, thinly sliced**
	salt
	pepper
	flat-leaf parsley sprigs, to garnish

1 Heat the butter and oil in a large frying pan. Add the chicken livers and cook over a high heat for 3–4 minutes, stirring, until browned on the outside but still light pink inside. Remove from the heat and stir in the vinegar and mustard. Season with salt and pepper to taste.

2 Arrange the salad leaves on 4 individual serving plates.

3 Spoon the hot chicken liver mixture on top of the salad leaves and sprinkle with the spring onions. Garnish with parsley sprigs and serve at once.

alcohol free	
citrus free	✔
dairy free	
gluten free	✔
wheat free	✔

herb salad with grilled haloumi

Serves 6 – Preparation time: 20 minutes – Cooking time: 8 minutes

Per serving – Energy: 217 kcals/895 kJ · Protein: 10 g · Carbohydrate: 2 g · Fat: 19 g · Fibre: 1 g

1	**Cos lettuce**
50 g	**(2 oz) rocket or young leaf spinach**
	handful of mixed herbs,
	such as dill, chervil, coriander,
	basil and parsley, roughly torn
250 g	**(8 oz) haloumi cheese**
1–2	**tablespoons olive oil**
2	**quantities Vinaigrette Dressing**
	(see page 75)
	pepper

1 Tear the lettuce into bite-sized pieces and place it in a large, shallow salad bowl with the rocket or leaf spinach and mixed herbs.

2 Cut the haloumi into small cubes less than 2.5 cm (1 inch). Place the cubes in a baking tin large enough to hold them in one layer, add the olive oil and season with pepper. Toss gently to coat the cheese then cook under a preheated hot grill for about 8 minutes, stirring occasionally, until golden brown on all sides. Scatter the haloumi over the salad. Add the dressing to the salad, toss well and serve immediately.

alcohol free	
citrus free	✔
dairy free	
gluten free	✔
wheat free	✔

roasted autumn vegetables with garlic sauce

Serves 4 – Preparation time: 25 minutes – Cooking time: 1¹/₂ hours

Per serving – Energy: 520 kcals/2165 kJ · Protein: 8 g · Carbohydrate: 54 g · Fat: 32 g · Fibre: 7 g

✔	alcohol free
✔	citrus free
	dairy free
	gluten free
	wheat free

1 large garlic bulb
2 large onions, cut into wedges
8 small carrots, quartered
12 small potatoes
2 fennel heads, thickly sliced
4 rosemary sprigs
4 thyme sprigs
6 tablespoons extra virgin olive oil
   salt
   pepper

Garlic Sauce:
1 large slice of day-old bread,
   about 75 g (3 oz)
4 tablespoons semi-skimmed milk
75 ml (3 fl oz) extra virgin olive oil

1 Blanch the whole garlic bulb in boiling water for 5 minutes. Drain and pat dry on kitchen paper.

2 Put all the vegetables and herbs into a large roasting tin, placing the garlic in the middle. Season well with salt and pepper and stir in the oil to coat the vegetables. Cover the pan with foil and roast in a preheated oven at 220°C (425°F), Gas Mark 7 for 50 minutes. Remove the foil and roast for a further 30 minutes.

3 To make the garlic sauce, remove the garlic bulb from the roasting tin. Discard the skin then mash the flesh with a fork. Put the bread into a bowl, add the milk and soak for 5 minutes.

4 Place the bread and garlic flesh in a food processor or blender and work to a smooth paste. Gradually blend in the oil until evenly combined then season to taste with salt and pepper. Serve the vegetables with the garlic sauce for dipping.

soda bread

Makes 1 loaf – Preparation time: about 10 minutes – Cooking time: 40–45 minutes

10 slices, per slice – Energy: 146 kcals/620 kJ · Protein: 5 g · Carbohydrate: 24 g · Fat: 4 g · Fibre: 1 g

50 g	**(2 oz) soya flour**
300 g	**(10 oz) brown rice flour**
¹/₂	**teaspoon salt**
³/₄	**teaspoon cream of tartar**
³/₄	**teaspoon bicarbonate of soda**
1	**tablespoon sunflower oil**
275 ml	**(9 fl oz) soya milk**

1 Put the flours, salt, cream of tartar and bicarbonate of soda into a bowl. Mix the oil with the soya milk and combine with the dry ingredients to form a soft dough.

2 Shape the dough into a round and place it on a greased baking sheet. Bake in a preheated oven at 200°C (400°F), Gas Mark 6 for 40–45 minutes until the loaf sounds hollow when tapped on the bottom. Cool on a wire rack.

alcohol free	✔
citrus free	✔
dairy free	✔
gluten free	✔
wheat free	✔

walnut and sultana bread

Makes 1 large loaf – Preparation time: 20 minutes, plus rising – Cooking time: 40 minutes

16 slices, per slice – Energy: 162 kcals/680 kJ · Protein: 6 g · Carbohydrate: 25 g · Fat: 5 g · Fibre: 2 g

15 g	**(¹/₂ oz) fresh yeast**
500 g	**(1 lb) granary flour, plus extra for dusting**
1	**teaspoon sugar**
300 ml	**(¹/₂ pint) warm water**
1	**teaspoon salt**
25 g	**(1 oz) butter**
50 g	**(2 oz) organic oats,**
	plus extra for sprinkling
50 g	**(2 oz) walnuts, roughly chopped**
50 g	**(2 oz) sultanas**
2	**tablespoons malt extract**
	vegetable oil, for greasing

1 Combine the yeast with 4 tablespoons of the flour, the sugar and half the water. Leave in a warm place for 10 minutes until frothy.

2 Mix together the remaining flour and the salt. Rub in the butter and stir in the oats, nuts and sultanas. Make a well in the centre and gradually add the yeasty water, malt extract and remaining water to form a stiff dough.

3 Turn out the dough on to a lightly floured surface and knead for 8–10 minutes until it is smooth and elastic. Place in an oiled bowl, turn once to coat the dough with oil, cover and leave to rise in a warm, draught-free place for about 45 minutes, or until doubled in size.

4 Knock back the dough by gently kneading it and shape it into an oval. Place on an oiled baking sheet, cover with oiled polythene and let rise for a further 20 minutes.

5 Brush the surface with water and scatter over the extra oats. Slash the top then bake in a preheated oven at 220°C (425°F), Gas Mark 7 for 35–40 minutes until the bread has risen and sounds hollow when tapped on the bottom. Leave to cool on a wire rack before slicing.

alcohol free	✔
citrus free	✔
dairy free	
gluten free	
wheat free	

steak with fresh tomato sauce

Serves 4 – Preparation time: 15 minutes – Cooking time: 16–20 minutes

Per serving – Energy: 304 kcals / 1273 kJ · Protein: 35 g · Carbohydrate: 5 g · Fat: 14 g · Fibre: 1 g

	alcohol free
✔	citrus free
✔	dairy free
✔	gluten free
✔	wheat free

1 x **150 g (5 oz) rump steaks, each about 2 cm (³/₄ inch) thick**
olive oil, for sprinkling and frying
125 ml **(4 fl oz) dry red wine**
salt
pepper
sautéed potato wedges, to serve

Tomato Sauce:

2 **tablespoons olive oil**
3 **garlic cloves, crushed**
500 g **(1 lb) plum tomatoes, skinned, deseeded and chopped**
handful of basil sprigs, plus extra to garnish

1 Beat the steaks with a rolling pin to tenderize them. Season with salt and pepper, sprinkle with oil and leave to stand.

2 To make the sauce, heat the oil in a saucepan and sauté the garlic for 1 minute. Add the tomatoes and season to taste with salt and pepper. Bring to the boil, then cook over a moderate heat for 5 minutes, until the tomatoes are just softened. Add the basil.

3 Oil a large frying pan and sauté the steaks over a moderate heat for 2 minutes on each side, until lightly browned. Add the red wine. Top each steak with a thick layer of the sauce, cover the pan tightly and cook over a low heat for 6–10 minutes or until the steaks are tender and cooked to your liking. Serve at once on a bed of sautéed potato wedges and garnish with basil sprigs.

pork in hot sauce

Serves 2 – Preparation time: about 20 minutes, plus marinating – Cooking time: 10 minutes

Per serving – Energy: 322 kcals/1340 kJ · Protein: 20 g · Carbohydrate: 8 g · Fat: 23 g · Fibre: 3 g

175 g   (6 oz) boned lean pork, shredded
2   spring onions, finely chopped
1   slice fresh root ginger, finely chopped
2   garlic cloves, finely chopped
1   tablespoon wheat-free soy sauce
1½   teaspoons cornflour
    vegetable oil, for deep-frying
250 g   (8 oz) aubergine, cut into
        diamond-shaped chunks
1   tablespoon Tabasco sauce
3–4   tablespoons stock or water
    chopped spring onions, to garnish

1 Put the pork into a bowl with the spring onions, ginger, garlic, soy sauce and cornflour. Mix well and leave to marinate for about 20 minutes.

2 Heat enough oil in a wok to deep-fry the aubergine. Lower the heat, add the aubergine and deep-fry for 1½ minutes. Remove the aubergine with a slotted spoon and drain on kitchen paper.

3 Pour off all but 1 tablespoon of the oil from the wok. Add the pork and stir-fry for 1 minute. Add the aubergine and Tabasco sauce and cook for about 1½ minutes. Moisten with the stock or water and simmer until the liquid has almost completely evaporated. Serve hot, garnished with chopped spring onions.

alcohol free	✔
citrus free	✔
dairy free	✔
gluten free	✔
wheat free	✔

chicken kebabs and marinated rice

Serves 4 – Preparation time: about 20 minutes, plus marinating – Cooking time: 40 minutes

Per serving – Energy: 397 kcals/1676 kJ · Protein: 33 g · Carbohydrate: 50 g · Fat: 9 g · Fibre: 5 g

200 g   (7 oz) brown rice
600 ml   (1 pint) water
1   tablespoon wine or cider vinegar
1   teaspoon clear honey
1   tablespoon sunflower oil
½   teaspoon ground ginger
2   carrots, sliced into julienne strips
500 g   (1 lb) boneless, skinless chicken
        breasts, cut into bite-sized pieces
4   baby onions, halved
250 g   (8 oz) mushrooms
1   tablespoon paprika
    Tabasco sauce
    salt
    pepper

1 Put the rice, water and a pinch of salt into a saucepan. Bring to the boil and stir once. Lower the heat, cover and simmer for 20–25 minutes, or according to packet instructions, until the rice is tender and the liquid absorbed. Remove from the heat and leave to cool.

2 To make the marinade, in a large bowl mix together the vinegar, honey, 1 teaspoon of the oil and the ground ginger with pepper to taste. Add the rice and carrots. Cover and leave to stand for 2 hours.

3 Thread the chicken, onions and mushrooms on to oiled skewers. Mix together the remaining oil, the paprika and a few drops of Tabasco sauce and brush over the kebabs. Grill under a preheated hot grill for 15 minutes, turning and basting occasionally. Serve with the marinated rice and carrots, reheated if you prefer a hot accompaniment.

alcohol free	
citrus free	✔
dairy free	✔
gluten free	✔
wheat free	✔

chicken-filled tortillas

Serves 4 – Preparation time: 30 minutes, plus marinating – Cooking time: 40 minutes

Per serving – Energy: 913 kcals/3823 kJ · Protein: 52 g · Carbohydrate: 77 g · Fat: 46 g · Fibre: 8 g

✔	alcohol free
	citrus free
	dairy free
	gluten free
	wheat free

6   skinless chicken breast fillets,
       cut into small pieces

2   tablespoons olive oil

2   large onions, sliced

1   red pepper, cored, deseeded and
       cut into strips

1   green pepper, cored, deseeded and
       cut into strips

12   soft tortillas, warmed

250 g   (8 oz) guacamole

300 ml   (¹/₂ pint) soured cream

2   tablespoons toasted sesame seeds

1   tablespoon chopped coriander

Marinade:

    juice of 4 limes

3   tablespoons olive oil

1   teaspoon dried oregano

1   teaspoon dried coriander

1 To make the marinade, combine the lime juice, olive oil, oregano and coriander in a bowl. Add the chicken, cover and refrigerate for 4 hours.

2 Put the chicken and marinade into a roasting tin, cover with foil and bake in a preheated oven at 200°C (400°F), Gas Mark 6 for 30 minutes, removing the foil for the last 10 minutes.

3 Meanwhile, heat the oil in a frying pan and sauté the onions and peppers. Place a little on each tortilla and top with the chicken, guacamole, soured cream and sesame seeds. Sprinkle with coriander and roll up the tortillas into cones. Serve at once.

chicken and broccoli risotto

Serves 4 – Preparation time: 15 minutes – Cooking time: about 40 minutes

Per serving – Energy: 524 kcals/2184 kJ · Protein: 26 g · Carbohydrate: 59 g · Fat: 20 g · Fibre: 1 g

250 g	**(8 oz) broccoli florets**
40 g	**(1¹/₂ oz) butter**
2	**tablespoons olive oil**
2	**skinless, boneless chicken breasts, diced**
¹/₂	**onion, very finely chopped**
1	**garlic clove, finely chopped**
1–2	**red chillies, deseeded and very finely chopped**
300 g	**(10 oz) arborio rice**
1 litre	**(1³/₄ pints) hot chicken stock**
3	**tablespoons freshly grated Parmesan cheese**
	salt
	pepper

1 Drop the broccoli florets into a pan of simmering water and cook for 3–4 minutes. Drain and set aside.

2 Heat 15 g (¹/₂ oz) of the butter with the oil in a large heavy-based pan. Add the chicken and stir-fry gently for 2–3 minutes. Add the onion and fry for 5 minutes until it is soft but not coloured. Add the garlic and chilli, and fry until the garlic is golden but not browned.

3 Add the rice to the pan and stir for 1–2 minutes. Add the hot stock, a ladleful at a time, stirring frequently and allowing the liquid to be absorbed before adding more. Continue to cook until all the stock has been absorbed. The process will take about 25 minutes, leaving the rice tender but still firm.

4 Add the broccoli florets to the rice with the Parmesan. Season with salt and pepper, stir in the remaining butter and serve.

alcohol free	✔
citrus free	✔
dairy free	
gluten free	✔
wheat free¹	✔

fettuccine with chanterelles

Serves 4 – Preparation time: 15 minutes – Cooking time: about 30 minutes

Per serving – Energy: 677 kcals/2755 kJ · Protein: 14 g · Carbohydrate: 50 g · Fat: 46 g · Fibre: 2 g

	alcohol free
✔	citrus free
	dairy free
✔	gluten free
✔	wheat free

300 g	**(10 oz) chanterelles, morels or other wild mushrooms**
500 ml	**(17 fl oz) chicken stock**
15 g	**(^{1}/$_{2}$ oz) butter**
1	**tablespoon olive oil**
1	**bunch of spring onions, finely chopped**
4	**tablespoons dry white wine**
300 g	**(10 oz) fresh fettuccine verde**
350 ml	**(12 fl oz) whipping cream or crème fraîche**
2	**tablespoons toasted pine nuts**
	salt
	pepper

1 Thinly slice the mushrooms, reserving any discarded pieces of stem or peel.

2 Pour the stock into a saucepan and bring to the boil. Add the mushroom peelings and cook over a moderately high heat until reduced to 125 ml (4 fl oz). Strain through a sieve and discard the mushroom peelings.

3 Melt the butter with the oil in a large frying pan. Add the mushrooms and spring onions and cook, stirring, until the mushrooms begin to give off their liquid. Add the wine and cook over a high heat until the liquid has nearly evaporated.

4 Bring a large saucepan of water to the boil. Add a generous pinch of salt. Cook the pasta according to the packet instructions until tender. Drain and keep warm.

5 Add the stock and the cream to the mushroom mixture. Bring to the boil and reduce the sauce to half its original volume. Season to taste. Add the drained pasta and pine nuts and toss to combine. Serve immediately.

caribbean black-eyed beans and rice

Serves 4 – Preparation time: 10 minutes, plus standing – Cooking time: 30 minutes

Per serving – Energy: 422 kcals/1775 kJ · Protein: 15 g · Carbohydrate: 76 g · Fat: 7 g · Fibre: 1 g

✔	alcohol free
✔	citrus free
✔	dairy free
✔	gluten free
✔	wheat free

2	**tablespoons sunflower oil**
1	**small onion, finely chopped**
1	**garlic clove, crushed**
1	**teaspoon grated fresh root ginger**
^{1}/$_{2}$	**teaspoon hot paprika**
^{1}/$_{4}$	**teaspoon pepper**
2	**tomatoes, skinned and chopped**
150 ml	**(^{1}/$_{4}$ pint) coconut milk**
250 g	**(8 oz) long-grain rice, rinsed**
425 g	**(14 oz) can black-eyed beans, drained**
600 ml	**(1 pint) vegetable stock**
1	**teaspoon salt**
	parsley sprigs, to garnish

1 Heat the oil in a large saucepan and fry the onion, garlic, ginger, paprika and black pepper for 5 minutes, stirring frequently. Add the tomatoes and coconut milk and simmer gently for 10 minutes.

2 Add the remaining ingredients and bring to the boil. Cover, reduce the heat to low and simmer for 15 minutes. Remove the saucepan from the heat and leave to stand for 10 minutes. Stir well, then taste and adjust the seasoning, if necessary. Serve garnished with parsley sprigs.

chilli tagliatelle

Serves 4 – Preparation time: about 10 minutes – Cooking time: 6–8 minutes

Per serving – Energy: 543 kcals/2193 kJ · Protein: 17 g · Carbohydrate: 60 g · Fat: 26 g · Fibre: 1 g

375 g	(12 oz) fresh tagliatelle verde
4	tablespoons olive oil
2	garlic cloves, crushed
2	red chillies, deseeded and chopped
50 g	(2 oz) button mushrooms, sliced
4	tablespoons balsamic vinegar
2	tablespoons orange juice
3	tablespoons ready-made red pesto
1	bunch of spring onions, shredded
25 g	(1 oz) toasted hazelnuts, chopped
	salt
	pepper

1 Bring a large pan of water to the boil. Add a generous pinch of salt. Cook the pasta according to packet instructions until tender.

2 Meanwhile, heat the oil in a large frying pan. Add the garlic, chillies and mushrooms and fry gently for 2 minutes. Reduce the heat and stir in the balsamic vinegar, orange juice, red pesto, spring onions and hazelnuts and heat through. Season to taste with salt and pepper.

3 Drain the pasta thoroughly and add it to the garlic and chilli mixture, tossing well. Serve at once.

alcohol free	✔
citrus free	
dairy free	
gluten free	
wheat free	

pappardelle with pesto and potatoes

Serves 4 – Preparation time: 15 minutes – Cooking time: about 20 minutes

Per serving – Energy: 699 kcals/2855 kJ · Protein: 24 g · Carbohydrate: 62 g · Fat: 40 g · Fibre: 1 g

375 g	(12 oz) new potatoes or large red-skinned potatoes, cut into chunks
2	tablespoons olive oil
1	tablespoon coarse sea salt
300 g	(10 oz) fresh pappardelle pasta
250 g	(8 oz) ready-made pesto
	salt
	mixed green salad, to serve (optional)

To Garnish:

2	tablespoons toasted pine nuts
2	tablespoons finely chopped parsley

1 Cook the potatoes in a pan of lightly salted boiling water for 15–20 minutes until just tender.

2 Drain the potatoes, dry them on kitchen paper, then put them into a shallow dish with the olive oil and coarse sea salt and toss gently to coat with the oil.

3 Meanwhile, bring a large pan of water to the boil. Add a generous pinch of salt. Cook the pasta according to packet instructions until tender.

4 Drain the pasta well and transfer to a warmed serving bowl. Add the potatoes and pesto and toss thoroughly. Garnish with the pine nuts and parsley, and serve with a mixed green salad, if liked.

alcohol free	✔
citrus free	✔
dairy free	
gluten free	
wheat free	

halibut aurora

Serves 4 — Preparation time: 20 minutes — Cooking time: 30–35 minutes

Per serving — Energy: 350 kcals/1465 kJ · Protein: 36 g · Carbohydrate: 2 g · Fat: 20 g · Fibre: 0 g

	alcohol free
✔	citrus free
	dairy free
✔	gluten free
✔	wheat free

625 g (1¹/₄ lb) tail piece of halibut, boned, skinned and divided into 4 fillets

300 ml (¹/₂ pint) dry white wine

1 shallot, chopped

¹/₂ teaspoon anchovy relish

¹/₂ teaspoon tomato purée

125 g (4 oz) cooked peeled prawns, thawed if frozen

4 tablespoons double cream

salt

pepper

green vegetables, to serve (optional)

1 Put the fish fillets into a large saucepan. Add the wine, shallot and salt and pepper to taste. Poach over a low heat for 5 minutes. Using a fish slice, lift the fish carefully into a greased ovenproof dish.

2 Add the anchovy relish, tomato purée and prawns to the fish poaching liquid in the saucepan and boil until reduced by half. Stir in the cream, heat until thickened, then pour it around the fish.

3 Transfer the dish to a preheated oven at 200°C (400°F), Gas Mark 6 and cook the halibut for 20 minutes. Serve immediately with steamed or boiled green vegetables, if liked.

baked halibut with rosemary

Serves 4 – Preparation time: 15 minutes – Cooking time: 15 minutes

Per serving – Energy: 322 kcals/1360 kJ · Protein: 46 g · Carbohydrate: 8 g · Fat: 12 g · Fibre: 3 g

2	tablespoons olive oil
4	halibut steaks, about 250 g (8 oz) each
125 g	(4 oz) shallots, finely chopped
750 g	(1¹/₂ lb) tomatoes, skinned and finely chopped
2	tablespoons chopped rosemary
	sea salt
	pepper
	rosemary sprigs, to garnish

1 Cut out 4 pieces of foil large enough to enclose the halibut steaks. Brush the foil with olive oil. Season both sides of the halibut steaks with salt and pepper and place them on the foil. Scatter the shallots over the fish, then arrange the tomatoes over the shallots. Sprinkle with the chopped rosemary. Drizzle the remaining olive oil over the halibut steaks and wrap up in the foil.

2 Put the parcels on a rack in a roasting tin and bake in a preheated oven at 180°C (350°F), Gas Mark 4 for 15 minutes. To serve, garnish the halibut steaks with sprigs of rosemary. New potatoes roughly mashed and sprinkled with parsley, and a crisp green salad would be good accompaniments.

alcohol free	✔
citrus free	✔
dairy free	✔
gluten free	✔
wheat free	✔

many tomato pizza

Serves 2 – Preparation time: 30 minutes, plus rising – Cooking time: 20 minutes

Per serving – Energy: 833 kcals/3496 kJ · Protein: 19 g · Carbohydrate: 105 g · Fat: 40 g · Fibre: 10 g

✔	alcohol free
	citrus free
✔	dairy free
	gluten free
	wheat free

Pizza Dough:

**250 g (8 oz) strong plain flour,
plus extra for dusting**

¹/₂ teaspoon salt

¹/₂ teaspoon fast-action dried yeast

125 ml (4 fl oz) warm water

**1 tablespoon extra virgin olive oil,
plus extra for oiling**

Topping:

2 large ripe plum tomatoes, sliced

125 g (4 oz) red cherry tomatoes, halved

125 g (4 oz) yellow pear tomatoes, halved

**4 sun-dried tomatoes in oil,
drained and halved**

handful of basil leaves, torn into pieces

2 teaspoons grated lemon rind

12 black olives, pitted

olive oil, for drizzling

sea salt

pepper

1 To make the dough, sift the flour and salt into a large bowl and stir in the dried yeast. Make a well in the centre and gradually stir in the water and oil to form a soft dough.

2 Turn out the dough on to a lightly floured surface and knead for 8–10 minutes until smooth and elastic. Place the dough in an oiled bowl, turn once to coat it with oil and cover with oiled clingfilm. Leave to rise in a warm, draught-free place for 45 minutes or until doubled in size.

3 Lightly knead the dough, divide it in half and roll each piece into a 23 cm (9 inch) round. Transfer to 2 oiled pizza plates or a large oiled baking sheet.

4 Dry the tomato slices on kitchen paper. Arrange all the tomatoes over the pizzas, then scatter with the basil, lemon rind and black olives. Season well and drizzle with a little olive oil.

5 Bake at the top of a preheated oven at 190°C (375°F), Gas Mark 5 for 20 minutes until the bases are crisp and the tops golden. Serve at once.

morels with wild rice

Serves 2 – Preparation time: 10 minutes, plus soaking – Cooking time: about 30 minutes

Per serving – Energy: 646 kcals/2695 kJ · Protein: 7 g · Carbohydrate: 62 g · Fat: 40 g · Fibre: 5 g

150 g	(5 oz) fresh morels, rinsed, trimmed and halved lengthways,
or 15 g	(½ oz) dried morels plus
	5 g (¼ oz) dried horn of plenty and
	125 g (4 oz) mixed fresh mushrooms, such as shiitake, yellow and grey oyster, trimmed
150 g	(5 oz) wild rice, well rinsed
50 g	(2 oz) butter
75 ml	(3 fl oz) double cream
1	tablespoon brandy
	salt
	pepper

1 If using dried mushrooms, soak them in a bowl of warm water for 20–30 minutes, then drain.

2 Place the wild rice in a saucepan of salted boiling water and cook for 18–20 minutes, or according to packet instructions, until the grains begin to split. Drain well.

3 Meanwhile, melt half the butter in a heavy-based frying pan, add all the mushrooms and sauté over a moderately high heat for 2½–3 minutes. Season to taste with salt and pepper, add the cream and brandy, then reduce the heat and continue cooking until the liquid has almost all evaporated. Transfer the mushrooms to a bowl, cover and keep warm.

4 Melt the remaining butter in the pan, add the wild rice and reheat, stirring to coat it well with the buttery juices. Season to taste and serve topped with the mushrooms.

alcohol free	
citrus free	✔
dairy free	
gluten free	✔
wheat free	✔

DESSERTS

rice with coconut milk

Serves 6 – Preparation time: 10–15 minutes, plus soaking – Cooking time: 30–40 minutes

Per serving – Energy: 458 kcals/1928 kJ · Protein: 8 g · Carbohydrate: 100 g · Fat: 3 g · Fibre: 1 g

✔ alcohol free
✔ citrus free
✔ dairy free
✔ gluten free
✔ wheat free

500 g	**(1 lb) glutinous rice**
400 ml	**(14 fl oz) canned coconut milk**
175 g	**(6 oz) sugar**
1	**tablespoon salt**

To Serve:
1 **mango, sliced**
2 **tablespoons dry-fried sesame seeds**

This Thai dessert is decorated with dry-fried sesame seeds, which provide a delicious crunchy contrast to the soft textures of the rice and mango. To dry-fry sesame seeds, put them into a wok or small frying pan over a gentle heat and toast for 3–4 minutes, stirring constantly, until golden. Dry-fried sesame can be stored in an air-tight container for 3–4 days.

1 Wash the rice, cover with water and soak for at least 3 hours. Drain thoroughly and spread out in a large steamer. Place over a large pan of simmering water and steam for 30–40 minutes.

2 Combine the coconut milk, sugar and salt in a large pan and bring gently to the boil, stirring constantly. When it boils, stir in the cooked rice, remove from the heat and cover the pan. Leave to stand for 15 minutes.

3 Spoon the rice on to serving plates and arrange a few slices of mango on the side. Sprinkle with the toasted sesame seeds and serve.

lemon pudding

Serves 4 – Preparation time: 20–30 minutes – Cooking time: 1³/₄ hours

Per serving – Energy: 615 kcals/2596 kJ · Protein: 8 g · Carbohydrate: 110 g · Fat: 19 g · Fibre: 2 g

75 g	(3 oz) butter, softened, plus extra for greasing
125 g	(4 oz) caster sugar
2	eggs, lightly beaten
2	tablespoons lemon marmalade
175 g	(6 oz) self-raising flour
75 ml	(3 fl oz) milk
	Sauce:
125 g	(4 oz) lemon marmalade
2	tablespoons sugar
250 ml	(8 fl oz) water
3	teaspoons grated lemon rind

alcohol free	✔
citrus free	
dairy free	
gluten free	
wheat free	

1 To make the pudding, beat the butter and sugar in a bowl until the mixture is light and fluffy and holds the trail of the beaters. Beat in the eggs and marmalade. Sift in the flour and add enough milk to make a mixture just soft enough to pour.

2 Grease a 1.5 litre (2¹/₂ pint) pudding basin and pour in the sponge mixture. Clip on the lid or cover with foil. Place in a steamer and set over a large pan of simmering water. Cover and cook for 1¹/₂ hours. Remove the pudding from the steamer.

3 To make the sauce, simmer the marmalade, sugar, water and rind in a pan for 10 minutes, or until thickened. Turn the pudding on to a serving plate and serve with the hot sauce.

champagne summer berries

Serves 4 – Preparation time: 15 minutes, plus chilling – Cooking time: 3–5 minutes

Per serving – Energy: 122 kcals/513 kJ · Protein: 2 g · Carbohydrate: 18 g · Fat: 0 g · Fibre: 8 g

250 g	(8 oz) strawberries, hulled and halved
250 g	(8 oz) raspberries
125 g	(4 oz) redcurrants
125 g	(4 oz) blueberries
25 g	(1 oz) caster sugar
4	tablespoons lemon juice
250 ml	(8 fl oz) chilled Champagne or sparkling white wine
	mint sprigs, to decorate

alcohol free	
citrus free	
dairy free	✔
gluten free	✔
wheat free	✔

1 Mix the berries together in a pudding basin. Sprinkle them with half the sugar and half the lemon juice. Set aside for 10 minutes.

2 Meanwhile, pour the remaining lemon juice and sugar on two large plates. Dip the rims of 4 glass dessert bowls into the lemon juice, shake off the excess, then dip each bowl into the sugar. The sugar will cling to the lemon juice, making an attractive frosted rim.

3 Cover the pudding basin with foil and tie in place with string. Place in a steamer and steam for 3–5 minutes.

4 To serve, spoon the fruit into the prepared dishes, being careful not to spoil the frosted rims. At the table, pour in the chilled Champagne and decorate with mint sprigs.

rhubarb, apple and double ginger crumble

Serves 8 – Preparation time: 20 minutes – Cooking time: 50 minutes

Per serving – Energy: 299 kcals/1256 kJ · Protein: 3 g · Carbohydrate: 46 g · Fat: 13 g · Fibre: 3 g

✔	alcohol free
✔	citrus free
	dairy free
	gluten free
	wheat free

125 g **(4 oz) plain flour**

50 g **(2 oz) ginger biscuits, crushed or ground in a food processor**

25 g **(1 oz) porridge oats**

100 g **(3¹/₂ oz) butter, plus extra for greasing**

3 **tablespoons light muscovado sugar**

500 g **(1 lb) rhubarb, chopped**

2 **tablespoons chopped preserved stem ginger, plus 2 tablespoons ginger syrup from the jar**

50 g **(2 oz) caster sugar**

4 **tablespoons water**

375 g **(12 oz) dessert apples, peeled, cored and sliced**

1 Sift the flour into a bowl and stir in the crushed biscuits and oats. Rub in the butter until the mixture resembles breadcrumbs, then stir in the muscovado sugar.

2 Place the rhubarb in a saucepan with the chopped ginger, ginger syrup, caster sugar and water. Heat gently, cover and simmer for 10 minutes.

3 Place the sliced apples in a greased pie dish. Add the rhubarb mixture and sprinkle over the crumble topping. Place in a preheated oven at 190°C (375°F), Gas Mark 5 and cook for 40 minutes until the filling is bubbling and the topping is golden. Serve hot.

pear and cardamom flan

Serves 6 – Preparation time: 20 minutes, plus chilling – Cooking time: 1 hour 20 minutes

Per serving – Energy: 605 kcals/2513 kJ · Protein: 8 g · Carbohydrate: 41 g · Fat: 46 g · Fibre: 2 g

175 g	**(6 oz) plain flour**
¹/₄	**teaspoon salt**
100 g	**(3¹/₂ oz) unsalted butter, diced, plus extra for greasing**
2	**tablespoons caster sugar**
1	**egg yolk**
1–2	**tablespoons cold water**
1	**teaspoon caster sugar, to serve (optional)**

Filling:

125 g	**(4 oz) unsalted butter, softened**
75 g	**(3 oz) caster sugar**
2	**small eggs, lightly beaten**
75 g	**(3 oz) ground hazelnuts**
25 g	**(1 oz) ground rice**
	seeds from 2 cardamom pods, crushed
1	**teaspoon grated lemon rind**
4	**tablespoons soured cream**
3	**small firm pears**

1 Sift the flour and salt into a bowl and rub in the butter until the mixture resembles fine breadcrumbs. Stir in the sugar and gradually work in the egg yolk and cold water to form a soft dough. Knead lightly, wrap in clingfilm and chill for 30 minutes.

2 Roll out the pastry on a lightly floured surface and use to line a greased 23 cm (9 inch) fluted flan tin. Prick the base with a fork and chill for a further 20 minutes.

3 Line the pastry case with nonstick baking paper and baking beans and bake in a preheated oven at 220°C (425°F), Gas Mark 7 for 10 minutes. Remove the paper and beans and bake for a further 10–12 minutes until the pastry is crisp and golden. Reduce the oven temperature to 180°C (350°F), Gas Mark 4.

4 To make the filling, beat together the butter and sugar in a bowl until pale and light then gradually beat in the eggs, a little at a time until incorporated. Lightly beat in all the remaining ingredients, except the pears. Pour the mixture into the prepared pastry case.

5 Peel and halve the pears and scoop out the cores. Thinly slice each pear lengthways, making sure that you keep the slices together. Then, using a palette knife, carefully transfer the sliced pears to the pastry case, arranging them neatly on the filling. Bake the flan for about 1 hour until golden and firm in the middle. Serve the flan warm, sprinkled with a little caster sugar, if liked.

alcohol free	✔
citrus free	
dairy free	
gluten free	
wheat free	

Eating a **nutritious, well-balanced diet** is something everybody should be doing. However, **people who suffer from headaches and migraines should pay special attention to their diets** because food and nutrition can play an important part in controlling their attacks.

A healthy diet should be low in saturated fats, high in fibre and contain at least five servings of fruit and vegetables every day. Headache and migraine sufferers should ensure they eat breakfast, even if it is only small, and **eat frequently throughout the day**. This is to help keep blood sugar levels steady. When blood sugar levels drop, they can trigger a headache or migraine. This may involve eating small snacks in between meals, and even eating a little something before bedtime to avoid waking with a headache.

The following recipes provide a good selection of choices for breakfast, lunch, dinner and snacks. They are packed with vitamins and minerals as well as other components of a healthy diet, and provide you with lots of opportunity to **improve your eating habits**. It is almost impossible to eat well all the time, but by making sure that you have some of these dishes every day you could help to manage your headaches and migraines more effectively.

banana shake

Serves 2 – Preparation time: 5 minutes

Per serving – Energy: 269 kcals/1142 kJ · Protein: 11 g · Carbohydrate: 48 g · Fat: 5 g · Fibre: 3 g

✔	alcohol free
✔	citrus free
	dairy free
✔	gluten free
✔	wheat free

2	bananas
600 ml	(1 pint) semi-skimmed milk
1	tablespoon clear honey, or to taste

1 Peel the bananas, then cut them into small pieces. Put them into a food processor or blender and work to a purée with the milk and honey.

2 To serve, pour into chilled glasses.

spiced fruit compôte

Serves 6 – Preparation time: 5 minutes, plus soaking and cooling – Cooking time: about 20 minutes

Per serving – Energy: 178 kcals/759 kJ · Protein: 3 g · Carbohydrate: 43 g · Fat: 1 g · Fibre: 11 g

✔	alcohol free
✔	citrus free
✔	dairy free
✔	gluten free
✔	wheat free

500 g	(1 lb) mixed dried fruit (apples, apricots, figs, peaches, prunes, sultanas)
300 ml	(½ pint) apple juice
300 ml	(½ pint) water
1	cinnamon stick
2	cloves

1 Put the dried fruit into a bowl and pour over the apple juice and water. Add the spices and leave to soak overnight. Alternatively, pour over boiling juice and water and soak for a few hours.

2 Transfer the fruit to a saucepan and bring to the boil. Lower the heat, cover and simmer for 20 minutes, or until the fruit is tender, adding more water if the syrup boils away. Leave to cool, then refrigerate until required.

strawberry and melon cups

Serves 4 – Preparation time: 8 minutes, plus chilling

Per serving – Energy: 99 kcals/417 kJ · Protein: 3 g · Carbohydrate: 18 g · Fat: 2 g · Fibre: 2 g

1	small honeydew or ogen melon, halved and deseeded
125 g	(4 oz) strawberries, hulled and sliced
5 cm	(2 inch) piece of cucumber, quartered and sliced
	finely grated rind and juice of 1 large orange
2	tablespoons chopped mint
15 g	(^{1}/₂ oz) split blanched pistachio nuts or roasted almonds
4–6	mint springs, to garnish

1 Cut the melon flesh into 1 cm (^{1}/₂ inch) cubes or scoop into balls. Reserve the shells intact. Place in a bowl with the strawberries and cucumber.

2 Mix the orange rind and juice with the mint and nuts. Fold gently into the salad.

3 Spoon the salad back into the melon shells, adding any orange juice from the bowl. Serve chilled, garnished with mint.

alcohol free	✔
citrus free	
dairy free	✔
gluten free	✔
wheat free	✔

oaty muesli

Serves 10 – Preparation time: 5 minutes

Per serving – Energy: 316 kcals/1332 kJ · Protein: 8 g · Carbohydrate: 54 g · Fat: 9 g · Fibre: 4 g

250 g	(8 oz) jumbo or rolled oats
125 g	(4 oz) barley or rye flakes
50 g	(2 oz) sesame seeds
50 g	(2 oz) sunflower seeds
125 g	(4 oz) seedless raisins or sultanas
25 g	(1 oz) pumpkin seeds
250 g	(8 oz) dried mixed fruit

Combine all the ingredients and store in an airtight container. Use as needed.

alcohol free	✔
citrus free	✔
dairy free	✔
gluten free	
wheat free	✔

breakfast squeak

Serves 6 – Preparation time: 8 minutes – Cooking time: 10 minutes

Per serving – Energy: 165 kcals/694 kJ · Protein: 5 g · Carbohydrate: 20 g · Fat: 8 g · Fibre: 7 g

500 g	(1 lb) potatoes, boiled and mashed
500 g	(1 lb) cabbage, shredded and cooked
2 x	300 g (10 oz) cans haricot beans, drained
25 g	(1 oz) margarine
2	tablespoons sunflower oil
	salt
	pepper

1 Mix together the potatoes, cabbage and beans. Beat in the margarine and salt and pepper to taste.

2 Heat the oil in a large frying pan, add the potato mixture and cook until the base is golden. Serve hot.

alcohol free	✔
citrus free	✔
dairy free	✔
gluten free	
wheat free	✔

caesar salad

Serves 4 – Preparation time: 20 minutes – Cooking time: 12 minutes

Per serving – Energy: 730 kcals/3033 kJ · Protein: 17 g · Carbohydrate: 41 g · Fat: 56 g · Fibre: 4 g

✔ alcohol free
✔ citrus free
  dairy free
  gluten free
  wheat free

1 Cos lettuce, separated into leaves
50 g (2 oz) can anchovies in olive oil, drained
1 small white loaf, thickly sliced
75 g (3 oz) butter, melted
3 tablespoons freshly grated
    Parmesan cheese

Dressing:
5 tablespoons mayonnaise
4–5 tablespoons water
1–2 garlic cloves
3 tablespoons finely grated
    Parmesan cheese
    coarse sea salt
    pepper

1 To make the dressing, put the mayonnaise in a bowl and stir in enough water to make a thin, pourable sauce. Crush the garlic to a paste with a little salt. Add to the mayonnaise with the Parmesan and stir. Thin with more water, if necessary, so the sauce remains pourable. Add pepper to taste.

2 Tear the lettuce leaves into large pieces and place in a shallow salad bowl. Snip the anchovies into small pieces and scatter over the lettuce.

3 Remove the crusts from the bread, brush the slices with melted butter and cut into 3 cm (1¼ inch) cubes. Brush a baking sheet with butter and arrange the bread cubes on it, brushing the cut sides with any remaining butter. Bake in a preheated oven at 200°C (400°F), Gas Mark 6 for about 12 minutes, or until crisp and golden. Watch them carefully as they colour quickly.

4 To serve, add the hot croûtons to the salad bowl and drizzle the dressing over the top. Sprinkle with Parmesan and serve.

lamb salad with minted yogurt

Serves 4 – Preparation time: 20 minutes – Cooking time: 3–4 minutes
Per serving – Energy: 290 kcals/1217 kJ · Protein: 34 g · Carbohydrate: 19 g · Fat: 9 g · Fibre: 5 g

3	**small carrots**
1	**small cauliflower**
425 g	**(14 oz) can pimientos**
¹/₂	**cucumber, peeled, deseeded and diced**
4	**spring onions, shredded**
375 g	**(12 oz) cold roast lamb, sliced**
	salt
	pepper
	mint leaves, to garnish

Dressing:

150 g	**(5 oz) natural yogurt**
2	**tablespoons mint jelly**

1 Using a potato peeler, pare the carrots into long thin strips or ribbons. Place in a bowl of iced water and leave to curl and crisp.

2 Divide the cauliflower into florets. Add to a saucepan of boiling water and cook for 3–4 minutes until barely tender. Drain and refresh under cold running water.

3 To make the dressing, mix the yogurt and mint jelly together until smooth. Season with salt and pepper.

4 Drain the pimientos and rinse thoroughly. Drain on kitchen paper and then slice thinly.

5 To serve the salad, put all the prepared ingredients together in a large bowl. Season and toss lightly. Drizzle over the dressing and garnish with a few mint leaves.

alcohol free	✔
citrus free	✔
dairy free	
gluten free	✔
wheat free	✔

chicory and pear salad with roquefort

Serves 4 – Preparation time: 15 minutes
Per serving – Energy: 318 kcals/1319 kJ · Protein: 10 g · Carbohydrate: 19 g · Fat: 23 g · Fibre: 1 g

2	**large ripe pears**
1	**tablespoon lemon juice**
1	**orange, segmented**
2	**chicory heads, separated into leaves**
175 g	**(6 oz) Roquefort cheese**
2	**tablespoons snipped chives**

Dressing:

3	**tablespoons walnut oil**
2	**tablespoons white wine vinegar**
¹/₂	**teaspoon finely grated orange rind**
	pinch of sugar
	salt
	pepper

1 To make the dressing, stir all the ingredients together in a small bowl or place them in a screw-top jar, close the lid tightly and shake until combined.

2 Peel, core and thinly slice the pears and place in a small bowl with the lemon juice. Toss well to prevent them from discolouring. Arrange the pear slices, orange segments and chicory leaves on individual plates or in a large shallow bowl. Pour over the dressing.

3 Just before serving, crumble the Roquefort over the salad and sprinkle with the chives.

alcohol free	✔
citrus free	
dairy free	
gluten free	✔
wheat free	✔

chicken and raisin salad

Serves 4 – Preparation time: 25 minutes, plus standing – Cooking time: about 12 minutes

Per serving – Energy: 526 kcals/2190 kJ · Protein: 40 g · Carbohydrate: 12 g · Fat: 36 g · Fibre: 3 g

alcohol free	
citrus free	
✔	dairy free
✔	gluten free
✔	wheat free

40 g   (1^1/$_2$ oz) raisins
4   tablespoons orange juice
pinch of ground cloves
1   teaspoon olive oil
50 g   (2 oz) blanched almonds, halved
500 g   (1 lb) cooked chicken, cut into strips
1   radicchio head, shredded
1   little gem lettuce, shredded
2   quantities Vinaigrette Dressing
     (see page 75)
salt
pepper
handful of chopped parsley, to garnish

1 Put the raisins, orange juice and ground cloves into a small saucepan, heat until boiling then remove from the heat. Leave to stand for about 30 minutes to plump up the raisins.

2 Heat the olive oil in a small saucepan over a moderate heat then brown the almonds, stirring constantly until golden.

3 Put the raisins, almonds, chicken strips and shredded salad leaves in a serving bowl. Toss and season well.

4 To serve, spoon over the dressing and scatter with chopped parsley.

smoked chicken and citrus salad

Serves 4 – Preparation time: 30 minutes

Per serving – Energy: 249 kcals/1044 kJ · Protein: 32 g · Carbohydrate: 14 g · Fat: 8 g · Fibre: 3 g

✔	alcohol free
	citrus free
	dairy free
✔	gluten free
✔	wheat free

375 g   (12 oz) boneless smoked chicken
1   pink grapefruit
2   small oranges
^{1}/$_2$ cucumber, thinly sliced
1   small fennel bulb, trimmed
     and thinly sliced (optional)
1   round lettuce, separated into leaves
50 g   (2 oz) frisée
50 g   (2 oz) lamb's lettuce or watercress
pink peppercorns (optional)

Yogurt Dressing:
150 ml   (^{1}/$_4$ pint) natural yogurt
1   tablespoon lemon juice
1   teaspoon clear honey
^{1}/$_2$ teaspoon Dijon mustard
salt
pepper

1 Carefully skin the smoked chicken and cut the flesh into bite-sized pieces. Place in a large bowl.

2 Using a small sharp knife, peel the grapefruit and oranges, taking care to remove all the pith. Working over a bowl to catch the juices, segment and roughly chop the flesh. Set the juice aside. Add the citrus fruit to the chicken with the cucumber and fennel, if using. Toss together lightly.

3 Arrange the chicken mixture and the salad leaves on 4 individual plates.

4 To make the yogurt dressing, put all the ingredients in a bowl and beat with a wooden spoon until smooth. Add salt and pepper to taste.

5 To serve, stir the reserved citrus juices and the pink peppercorns, if using, into the dressing and pour it over the salad.

chicory, orange and pasta salad

Serves 4 – Preparation time: 20 minutes – Cooking time: 5–10 minutes

Per serving – Energy: 682 kcals/2765 kJ · Protein: 20 g · Carbohydrate: 107 g · Fat: 21 g · Fibre: 6 g

500 g (1 lb) fresh tagliatelle
4 chicory heads, sliced
6 large oranges, segmented
2 tablespoons chopped tarragon
4 tablespoons snipped chives
salt

Orange Dressing:
6 tablespoons olive oil
2 tablespoons orange juice
2 tablespoons lemon juice
$^{1}/_{2}$ teaspoon coarsegrain mustard
1 teaspoon clear honey
1 teaspoon mixed herbs
1 teaspoon finely grated orange rind

1 Cut the tagliatelle into short strips. Bring a large pan of water to the boil. Add a generous pinch of salt. Cook the pasta according to packet instructions, until just tender. Drain well, rinse under cold water in a colander and drain again.

2 To make the orange dressing, mix together all the ingredients and pour over the pasta. Stir in the chicory, orange segments and herbs. Transfer to a serving dish and serve immediately.

alcohol free	✔
citrus free	
dairy free	✔
gluten free	
wheat free	

winter radish salad

Serves 4 – Preparation time: 20 minutes – Cooking time: about 3 minutes

Per serving – Energy: 174 kcals/726 kJ · Protein: 3 g · Carbohydrate: 19 g · Fat: 10 g · Fibre: 3 g

✔	alcohol free
	citrus free
✔	dairy free
✔	gluten free
✔	wheat free

125 g	(4 oz) cranberries, fresh or frozen
4	teaspoons caster sugar
375 g	(12 oz) winter radish (mooli)
75 g	(3 oz) baby spinach
	or watercress, washed and trimmed
2	small oranges, thinly sliced
200 g	(7 oz) can pimientos, drained
	and chopped
	salt
	pepper
1	quantity Vinaigrette Dressing
	(see page 75)

1 Place the cranberries and sugar in a small saucepan. Cook over a fairly high heat, stirring, for a few minutes until the sugar has dissolved and the cranberries begin to 'pop'. Remove from the heat and leave to cool.

2 Cut the radish into julienne strips. Arrange on 4 individual serving plates with the spinach or watercress, oranges and pimientos. Season with salt and pepper.

3 Just before serving, spoon the dressing over the salads and top with the prepared cranberries.

spinach and goats' cheese salad

Serves 4 — Preparation time: 15 minutes — Cooking time: about 3 minutes

Per serving — Energy: 345 kcals/1430 kJ · Protein: 10 g · Carbohydrate: 12 g · Fat: 29 g · Fibre: 3 g

175 g	**(6 oz) baby spinach**
2	**oranges, segmented**
175 g	**(6 oz) goats' cheese, diced**
5	**tablespoons olive oil**
50 g	**(2 oz) hazelnuts, roughly chopped**
1	**garlic clove, crushed**
5	**tablespoons orange juice**
1	**bunch of watercress, leaves stripped from the stalks and finely chopped**
2	**tablespoons chopped mixed herbs (parsley, tarragon, mint, dill, basil)**
	salt
	pepper

1 Combine the spinach leaves, oranges and goats' cheese in a large salad bowl.

2 Heat the olive oil in a small frying pan. Add the hazelnuts and garlic and cook for 1–2 minutes. Stir in the orange juice, watercress and herbs. Heat through, then quickly pour the hot dressing on to the salad. Add salt and pepper to taste, toss well and serve immediately.

alcohol free	✔
citrus free	
dairy free	
gluten free	✔
wheat free	✔

noodles in spicy broth

Serves 4 – Preparation time: 15 minutes – Cooking time: 15 minutes

Per serving – Energy: 558 kcals/2349 kJ · Protein: 28 g · Carbohydrate: 72 g · Fat: 19 g · Fibre: 5 g

alcohol free
✔ citrus free
✔ dairy free
gluten free
wheat free

250 g	(8 oz) cooked peeled prawns
1	teaspoon cornflour
1	tablespoon cold water
375 g	(12 oz) egg noodles
600 ml	(1 pint) boiling chicken stock
2	tablespoons light soy sauce
3	tablespoons vegetable oil
2	spring onions, thinly shredded
125 g	(4 oz) bamboo shoots or button mushrooms, thinly sliced
125 g	(4 oz) spinach leaves or Chinese leaves, thinly sliced
2	tablespoons dry sherry
1–2	teaspoons sesame oil
	salt

To Garnish:
1 red chilli, chopped
coriander sprigs

1 Put the prawns in a bowl with a pinch of salt. Mix the cornflour to a paste with the water and stir in.

2 Fill a large saucepan with lightly salted water and bring to the boil. Add the egg noodles and cook according to packet instructions until just tender. Drain well and place in a warmed serving bowl. Pour the stock over the noodles with half the soy sauce. Keep warm.

3 Heat the oil in a pan and add the spring onions. Add the prawns, the bamboo shoots or mushrooms and the spinach or Chinese leaves. Stir a few times, and then add 1 1/2 teaspoons salt, the remaining soy sauce and the sherry. Cook for 1–2 minutes, stirring constantly.

4 Pour the mixture over the noodles and sprinkle with sesame oil. Garnish with chilli and coriander sprigs.

kedgeree

Serves 4 – Preparation time: 10 minutes – Cooking time: 15–20 minutes

Per serving – Energy: 498 kcals/2083 kJ · Protein: 35 g · Carbohydrate: 51 g · Fat: 17 g · Fibre: 1 g

✔ alcohol free
✔ citrus free
dairy free
✔ gluten free
✔ wheat free

500 g	(1 lb) smoked haddock fillets
	milk, for poaching
50 g	(2 oz) butter
1	small onion or 2–3 spring onions, finely chopped
250 g	(8 oz) long-grain rice, cooked according to packet instructions
4	tablespoons finely chopped flat-leaf parsley
4	hard-boiled eggs, chopped
	salt
	pepper

To Garnish:
spring onions
hard-boiled egg wedges

1 Place the haddock in a large heavy-based pan and add enough milk to cover. Simmer gently for 10–15 minutes. Remove the skin and flake the fish. Reserve the milk.

2 Melt the butter in the pan. Add the onion or spring onions and cook gently until soft but not coloured. Add the rice and stir to heat it through.

3 Add the flaked haddock, taking care not to break up the flesh too much. Gently stir in the parsley and enough reserved milk to moisten the mixture, then add the chopped hard-boiled eggs. Season to taste with salt and pepper and turn into a warmed shallow serving dish. Garnish with spring onions and wedges of hard-boiled egg.

tuna fish cakes

Serves 4 – Preparation time: 10–15 minutes, plus chilling – Cooking time: about 12 minutes

Per serving – Energy: 382 kcals/1598 kJ · Protein: 27 g · Carbohydrate: 22 g · Fat: 21 g · Fibre: 2 g

300 g	**(10 oz) potatoes, boiled**
25 g	**(1 oz) butter or margarine**
300 g	**(10 oz) canned tuna, drained and flaked**
2	**tablespoons chopped parsley**
2	**eggs, beaten**
75 g	**(3 oz) breadcrumbs**
	oil, for shallow-frying
	salt
	pepper
	tomato salad, to serve

1 Mash the potatoes in a bowl with the butter or margarine, then mix in the tuna, parsley, salt and pepper to taste and half of the beaten egg. Cover the mixture and chill in the refrigerator for 20 minutes.

2 Place the tuna mixture on a floured surface and shape into a roll. Cut into 8 slices and shape each one into a flat round, about 6 cm (2¹/₂ inches) in diameter. Dip into the remaining egg, then coat with breadcrumbs.

3 Heat the oil in a frying pan. Add the fish cakes and fry for 2–3 minutes on each side, or until golden brown and heated through. Serve with a tomato salad.

alcohol free	✔
citrus free	✔
dairy free	
gluten free	
wheat free	

green bean and vegetable soup with pesto

Serves 4 – Preparation time: 15 minutes – Cooking time: 45 minutes

Per serving – Energy: 324 kcals/1350 kJ · Protein: 14 g · Carbohydrate: 14 g · Fat: 24 g · Fibre: 5 g

✔ alcohol free
✔ citrus free
✔ dairy free
✔ gluten free
✔ wheat free

2	**tablespoons extra virgin olive oil**
1	**leek, sliced**
2	**garlic cloves, crushed**
1	**potato, diced**
1	**celery stick, sliced**
1	**tablespoon chopped thyme**
425 g	**(14 oz) can flageolet beans**
600 ml	**(1 pint) vegetable stock**
1	**courgette, diced**
50 g	**(2 oz) green beans, halved**
125 g	**(4 oz) frozen broad beans, thawed**
150 ml	**(¹/₄ pint) ready-made pesto sauce**
	salt
	pepper

This wonderfully aromatic soup is a classic from the south of France, where it is known as *soupe au pistou*. It is served with fragrant pesto sauce, which is spooned into the soup as it is served.

1 Heat the oil in a large saucepan and fry the leek and garlic for 5 minutes. Add the potato, celery and thyme and fry for 10 minutes until lightly golden.

2 Stir in the flageolet beans with their liquid and the vegetable stock. Return to the boil, cover and simmer gently for 20 minutes. Add the courgette, green beans and broad beans and cook for 10 minutes. Add salt and pepper to taste.

3 Serve the soup in large bowls. Stir in a spoonful of pesto and serve at once.

chickpea, pasta and spinach soup

Serves 6 – Preparation time: 10 minutes – Cooking time: about 1 hour

Per serving – Energy: 256 kcals/1080 kJ · Protein: 14 g · Carbohydrate: 36 g · Fat: 7 g · Fibre: 8 g

2	**tablespoons extra virgin olive oil**
2	**garlic cloves, crushed**
1	**onion, chopped**
1	**tablespoon chopped rosemary**
2 x	**400 g (13 oz) cans chickpeas**
1.2 l	**(2 pints) vegetable stock**
75 g	**(3 oz) small pasta shapes**
125 g	**(4 oz) spinach, shredded**
	salt
	pepper

To Serve:
grated nutmeg
croûtons
freshly grated Parmesan cheese

1 Heat the oil in a large saucepan and fry the garlic, onion and rosemary over a low heat for 5 minutes until softened but not coloured. Add the chickpeas with their liquid and the vegetable stock, bring to the boil, cover and simmer for 30 minutes.

2 Add the pasta, return to the boil and simmer for 6–8 minutes.

3 Stir in the spinach and continue cooking for a further 5 minutes until both the pasta and spinach are tender. Season to taste with salt and pepper and serve at once, sprinkled with nutmeg, croûtons and grated Parmesan.

alcohol free	✔
citrus free	✔
dairy free	
gluten free	
wheat free	

bulgar wheat with tomato, broad beans, feta and mint

Serves 4 – Preparation time: 15 minutes, plus standing and cooling – Cooking time: 1 minute

Per serving – Energy: 599 kcals/2496 kJ · Protein: 22 g · Carbohydrate: 60 g · Fat: 31 g · Fibre: 5 g

250 g	(8 oz) bulgar wheat
475 ml	(16 fl oz) boiling water
250 g	(8 oz) frozen broad beans
1/2	cucumber
1	small red onion, chopped
4	tomatoes, chopped
2	tablespoons finely chopped mint
250 g	(8 oz) feta cheese
	salt
	pepper

Dressing:

6	tablespoons extra virgin olive oil
2	tablespoons wine vinegar
1	garlic clove, crushed
1/2	teaspoon sugar

1 Put the bulgar wheat into a large bowl and pour over the boiling water. Stir well and leave to stand for about 30 minutes until all the water is absorbed. Transfer to a serving dish and allow to cool.

2 Meanwhile, put the frozen broad beans into a pan of boiling water for 1 minute to blanch. Drain, rinse under cold running water and then drain well. Remove the waxy outer skins of the broad beans with your fingers, reserving the bright green beans inside. Add these to the bulgar wheat in the serving dish.

3 Peel the cucumber and cut it in half lengthways. Scoop out the seeds with a teaspoon. Slice or dice the cucumber and add to the salad with the red onion, tomato and mint. Season well with salt and pepper and toss lightly to mix.

4 Crumble or dice the feta cheese and sprinkle over the salad.

5 Whisk all the dressing ingredients together in a small bowl or place in a screw-top jar and shake until combined. Just before serving, pour the dressing over the salad and toss lightly.

pasta primavera

Serves 4 – **Preparation time: 10 minutes** – **Cooking time: 30 minutes**

Per serving – Energy: 557 kcals/2340 kJ · Protein: 17 g · Carbohydrate: 78 g · Fat: 22 g · Fibre: 22 g

375 g	**(12 oz) spaghetti**
250 g	**(8 oz) mangetout, trimmed**
250 g	**(8 oz) asparagus**
175 g	**(6 oz) thin green beans**
1	**carrot, cut into thin strips**
25 g	**(1 oz) unsalted butter**
4	**tablespoons olive oil**
1	**red pepper, cored, deseeded and diced**
2	**tablespoons pine nuts, toasted**
¹/₂	**small lettuce, shredded**
2	**tablespoons snipped chives**
	salt

To Garnish:

4	**tablespoons finely chopped parsley**
	freshly grated Parmesan cheese

1 Bring a large pan of water to the boil. Add a generous pinch of salt. Cook the pasta according to packet instructions until just tender. Drain the pasta, reserving the cooking water. Set the cooked pasta aside and keep warm.

2 Return the pasta cooking water to the boil and blanch the green vegetables and carrots separately, removing each one to iced water as soon as it is tender but still crisp, to stop the cooking. Drain well and pat dry with kitchen paper.

3 Melt the butter with the olive oil in a large frying pan over a moderate heat. Add the red pepper and sauté for 1 minute. Add the pine nuts and sauté for 1 further minute. Add the blanched vegetables and toss until they are well coated with oil and warmed through.

4 Place the cooked pasta in a warmed serving bowl. Add the hot vegetables with the shredded lettuce and chives and toss well. Add salt to taste and toss again. Garnish with parsley, sprinkle with Parmesan and serve immediately.

thai steamed fish curry

Serves 4 – Preparation time: 10 minutes – Cooking time: 15 minutes

Per serving – Energy: 168 kcals/708 kJ · Protein: 25 g · Carbohydrate: 5 g · Fat: 6 g · Fibre: 0 g

✔ alcohol free
✔ citrus free
dairy free
✔ gluten free
✔ wheat free

3 **tablespoons Thai red curry paste**
200 ml **(7 fl oz) coconut milk**
1 **tablespoon Thai fish sauce**
1 **egg, beaten**
500 g **(1 lb) skinless cod or halibut fillets,**
   cut into 5 cm (2 inch) pieces
1 **tablespoon chopped coriander**
1 **tablespoon chopped mint**
1 **tablespoon Thai sweet basil**
4 **kaffir lime leaves, finely sliced**
1 **large green chilli, deseeded**
   and finely sliced
1 **large red chilli, deseeded**
   and finely sliced
   plain boiled rice, to serve

1 Mix together the Thai red curry paste, coconut milk, fish sauce and beaten egg. Set aside.

2 Place the fish pieces in a shallow non-metallic dish. Add the coriander, mint and Thai sweet basil and mix gently. Pour the curry paste mixture over the fish and stir to coat evenly.

3 Scatter the kaffir lime leaves and chilli slices over the fish. Cover the dish with foil and steam over boiling water for 15 minutes, or until the fish is just cooked through. The sauce should be lightly thickened due to the addition of the egg. Serve immediately with the rice.

rainbow trout with lemon and ginger stuffing

Serves 6 – Preparation time: 20 minutes – Cooking time: 1 hour

Per serving – Energy: 507 kcals/2119 kJ · Protein: 31 g · Carbohydrate: 51 g · Fat: 20 g · Fibre: 4 g

375 g	**(12 oz) wild rice**
75 g	**(3 oz) pine nuts, toasted and chopped**
3	**tablespoons finely snipped chives, plus extra to garnish**
3	**bunches of spring onions, finely sliced**
75 g	**(3 oz) piece of fresh root ginger, peeled and grated**
	grated rind and juice of 2 lemons
6	**rainbow trout, gutted and cleaned**
50 g	**(2 oz) butter, softened**
	salt
	pepper
	strips of lemon rind, to garnish

1 Cook the wild rice in a large saucepan of boiling salted water for 40–45 minutes, or according to packet instructions, until tender. Drain thoroughly.

2 Turn the rice into a large bowl, add the toasted pine nuts, chives, spring onions, ginger and lemon rind. Season to taste with salt and pepper and stuff the trout with the mixture,

3 Line a baking sheet with a large piece of foil, allowing sufficient to fold over the top comfortably. Spread the butter over the foil. Put the trout on top and pour over the lemon juice. Fold the foil over the trout and fold the edges together to seal. Bake in a preheated oven at 200°C (400°F), Gas Mark 6 for 15 minutes until cooked through. Serve immediately, garnished with chives and strips of lemon rind.

alcohol free	✔
citrus free	
dairy free	
gluten free	✔
wheat free	✔

lemon sole with oranges and rice

Serves 4 – Preparation time: 10–15 minutes – Cooking time: 45 minutes

Per serving – Energy: 598 kcals/2522 kJ · Protein: 28 g · Carbohydrate: 76 g · Fat: 17 g · Fibre: 5 g

	alcohol free
	citrus free
	dairy free
✔	gluten free
✔	wheat free

250 g	(8 oz) wild rice
25 g	(1 oz) butter
4	shallots, finely chopped
300 ml	(½ pint) dry white wine
250 ml	(8 fl oz) orange juice
2	teaspoons grated orange rind
3	teaspoons redcurrant jelly (optional)
	clear honey, to taste
8	lemon sole fillets
2	tablespoons flour
	sunflower oil, for shallow-frying
2	oranges, cut into segments
	salt
	pepper
2	tablespoons chopped parsley, to garnish

1 Cook the wild rice in a large saucepan of boiling salted water for 40–45 minutes, or according to packet instructions, until tender.

2 Meanwhile, melt the butter in a large saucepan, add the shallots and cook for 3 minutes. Add the wine, orange juice, orange rind and redcurrant jelly, if using. Boil until reduced by half. Season with salt and pepper and add honey to taste. Cover and keep warm.

3 Coat the fish with flour and season well. Heat the oil in a frying pan, add the fish in batches and cook for 3 minutes on each side. Keep warm.

4 Drain the rice and stir in the orange segments. Spoon on to a warmed serving dish and place the fish on top. Pour the sauce over the fish and garnish with parsley.

sweet 'n' sour cod cutlets

Serves 4 – Preparation time: 10 minutes – Cooking time: 15–20 minutes

Per serving – Energy: 230 kcals/980 kJ · Protein: 31 g · Carbohydrate: 18 g · Fat: 4 g · Fibre: 0 g

✔	alcohol free
	citrus free
	dairy free
✔	gluten free
✔	wheat free

4	cod cutlets or steaks, about 175–200 g (6–7 oz) each
15 g	(½ oz) margarine
1	onion, thinly sliced
150 ml	(¼ pint) light fish stock
150 ml	(¼ pint) orange juice
2	tablespoons wine vinegar
1	tablespoon soy sauce
2	teaspoons soft brown sugar
1½	tablespoons cornflour

To Garnish:
julienne strips of orange rind, blanched
spring onions

1 Place the pieces of cod in a pan large enough to hold them in a single layer. Just cover with cold water and bring slowly to the boil over a moderate heat. Poach gently for about 10 minutes, or until the fish is tender.

2 Meanwhile, melt the margarine in a pan and sauté the onion for 5–7 minutes until soft but not coloured. Add the stock, orange juice, vinegar, soy sauce and sugar to the pan and stir well to combine. In a small bowl, blend the cornflour with a little water to make a creamy paste and add to the sauce. Bring to the boil, stirring, until the sauce is thickened. Simmer for 3–5 minutes.

3 When the fish is cooked, drain and place it in a warmed serving dish. Pour the sauce over the top and garnish with orange rind and spring onions.

stuffed fillets of fish with stir-fried vegetables

Serves 2 – Preparation time: 15 minutes – Cooking time: 20 minutes

Per serving – Energy: 308 kcals/1286 kJ · Protein: 34 g · Carbohydrate: 11 g · Fat: 15 g · Fibre: 2 g

4   plaice fillets, skinned
salt and pepper

Stuffing:
75 g   (3 oz) curd cheese or low-fat
       soft cheese
1   tablespoon chopped parsley
finely grated rind of ¹/₂ lime
1   tablespoon water

Stir-fry:
1   tablespoon sunflower oil
1   onion, sliced
2   carrots, cut into matchsticks
2   courgettes, cut into matchsticks
1   small fennel bulb or 2 celery sticks,
       cut into strips
50 g   (2 oz) button mushrooms, thinly sliced

To Garnish:
snipped chives
lime wedges

1 To make the stuffing, mix together the cheese, parsley, lime rind and water. Divide the mixture among the plaice fillets and spread it over the skinned side. Roll up the fillets and place them side-by-side in a small ovenproof dish. Cover the fish with foil and bake in a preheated oven at 180°C (350°F), Gas Mark 4 for about 20 minutes until cooked through.

2 Meanwhile, heat the oil in a wok or large frying pan over a high heat. Add the onion, carrots, courgettes, fennel or celery and mushrooms and cook for 2–3 minutes, stirring and turning constantly, until the vegetables are almost tender. Arrange them around the fish and serve garnished with chives and lime wedges.

alcohol free	✔
citrus free	
dairy free	
gluten free	✔
wheat free	✔

vegetable biryani

Serves 4 – Preparation time: 25 minutes – Cooking time: about 1 hour

Per serving – Energy: 650 kcals/2720 kJ · Protein: 17 g · Carbohydrate: 84 g · Fat: 28 g · Fibre: 8 g

✔ alcohol free
✔ citrus free
  dairy free
✔ gluten free
✔ wheat free

250 g	(8 oz) basmati rice, rinsed
6	tablespoons sunflower oil
2	large onions, thinly sliced
2	garlic cloves, crushed
2	teaspoons grated fresh root ginger
250 g	(8 oz) sweet potato, diced
2	large carrots, diced
1	tablespoon curry paste
2	teaspoons turmeric
1	teaspoon ground cinnamon
1	teaspoon chilli powder
300 ml	(½ pint) vegetable stock
4	ripe tomatoes, skinned, deseeded and diced
175 g	(6 oz) cauliflower florets
125 g	(4 oz) frozen peas, thawed
50 g	(2 oz) cashew nuts
2	tablespoons chopped fresh coriander
	salt
	pepper
2	hard-boiled eggs, quartered, to garnish

1 Bring a large saucepan of salted water to a rolling boil. Add the basmati rice and return to a simmer. Cook gently for 5 minutes. Drain, refresh under cold water and drain again. Spread the rice on a large baking sheet and set aside to dry.

2 Heat 2 tablespoons of the oil in a frying pan. Add half the onion and fry over a moderate heat for 10 minutes until very crisp and golden. Remove and drain on kitchen paper. Reserve for garnishing.

3 Add the remaining oil to the pan and fry the remaining onion with the garlic and ginger for 5 minutes. Add the potato, carrots and spices and continue to fry for a further 10 minutes until lightly golden.

4 Add the vegetable stock and tomatoes, bring to the boil, cover and simmer gently for 20 minutes. Add the cauliflower and peas and cook for a further 8–10 minutes until all the vegetables are tender.

5 Stir in the rice, cashew nuts, coriander and salt and pepper. Cook, stirring, for 3 minutes, then cover and remove from the heat. Leave to stand for 5 minutes before serving. Garnish with crispy onion slices and egg quarters.

green lentil and vegetable tagine with couscous

Serves 4 – Preparation time: 40–45 minutes, plus soaking – Cooking time: 40 minutes

Per serving – Energy: 518 kcals/2180 kJ · Protein: 17 g · Carbohydrate: 87 g · Fat: 14 g · Fibre: 10 g

125 g	(4 oz) green lentils
600 ml	(1 pint) water
4	tablespoons extra virgin olive oil
2	small onions
2	garlic cloves, chopped
1	tablespoon ground coriander
2	teaspoons ground cumin
1	teaspoon turmeric
1	teaspoon ground cinnamon
12	new potatoes, halved if large
2	large carrots, thickly sliced
250 g	(8 oz) couscous
2	courgettes, sliced
175 g	(6 oz) button mushrooms
300 ml	('/₂ pint) tomato juice
1	tablespoon tomato purée
125 g	(4 oz) ready-to-eat dried apricots, chopped
2	tablespoons chilli sauce, plus extra to serve (optional)

1 Put the lentils in a saucepan with the water. Bring to the boil, cover and simmer for 20 minutes.

2 Meanwhile, heat half the oil in a large saucepan and fry the onions, garlic and spices for 5 minutes. Add the potatoes and carrots and fry for a further 5 minutes. Add the lentils with their cooking liquid, cover and simmer gently for 15 minutes.

3 Rinse the couscous several times under cold running water to moisten all the grains, and spread out on a large baking sheet. Sprinkle over a little water then leave to soak for 15 minutes.

4 Heat the remaining oil in a frying pan and fry the courgettes and mushrooms for 4–5 minutes until lightly golden. Add to the lentil mixture with the tomato juice, tomato purée, dried apricots and chilli sauce and return to the boil. Cook for a further 10 minutes until the vegetables and lentils are tender.

5 Steam the couscous according to the packet instructions or over the stew in a double boiler for 6–7 minutes. Transfer to a large warmed platter, spoon on the vegetable and lentil tagine and serve the juices separately, with extra chilli sauce if liked.

alcohol free	✔
citrus free	✔
dairy free	✔
gluten free	✔
wheat free	✔

mozzarella and plum tomato lasagne with chilli

Serves 4 – Preparation time: 10 minutes – Cooking time: 20–30 minutes

Per serving – Energy: 339 kcals/1422 kJ · Protein: 17 g · Carbohydrate: 29 g · Fat: 18 g · Fibre: 4 g

✔	alcohol free
✔	citrus free
	dairy free
✔	gluten free
✔	wheat free

butter, for greasing

6 lasagne verde sheets, cooked

10 large plum tomatoes

125 g (4 oz) mozzarella cheese, sliced

125 g (4 oz) goats' cheese, sliced

1 small bunch of oregano, chopped
   a few drops of chilli-flavoured oil
   salt

1 Line a buttered 1.2 litre (2 pint) ovenproof dish with 2 sheets of lasagne, cutting them to fit if necessary. Slice 6 of the tomatoes and arrange half of them over the lasagne, packing them in well. Sprinkle with salt and add a few slices of mozzarella and goats' cheese and some oregano. Put 2 more sheets of lasagne on top and cover with the remaining tomato slices, half the remaining cheese slices and the remaining oregano. Top with the 2 remaining lasagne sheets.

2 Cut the remaining tomatoes into wedges, and scatter over the pasta with the rest of the cheese. Drizzle with the chilli-flavoured oil and bake in a preheated oven at 200°C (400°F), Gas Mark 6 for 20–30 minutes. Remove from the oven and leave to rest for 10 minutes before serving.

baked pasta with pepper sauce

Serves 4 – Preparation time: 20 minutes – Cooking time: 35 minutes

Per serving – Energy: 516 kcals/2184 kJ · Protein: 26 g · Carbohydrate: 79 g · Fat: 13 g · Fibre: 8 g

2	**large yellow peppers, cored, deseeded and finely chopped**
¹/₂	**onion, thinly sliced**
6	**plum tomatoes, skinned and chopped**
250 ml	**(8 fl oz) vegetable stock**
375 g	**(12 oz) penne or other dried pasta shapes**
¹/₂	**teaspoon chopped basil**
200 g	**(7 oz) mozzarella cheese, diced**
3	**tablespoons milk**
	salt
	pepper
	shredded basil leaves, to garnish

1 Place the peppers in a saucepan with the onion, tomatoes and a pinch of salt; cover and simmer for about 20 minutes, adding the stock after 5 minutes.

2 Bring a large pan of water to the boil. Add a generous pinch of salt. Cook the pasta according to packet instructions until just tender, then drain thoroughly.

3 Sprinkle the basil over the pepper sauce, adjust the seasoning to taste, then mix with the drained pasta and the diced mozzarella. Transfer to a large ovenproof dish, pour over the milk and bake in a preheated oven at 200°C (400°F), Gas Mark 6 for about 15 minutes, or until golden brown. To serve, garnish with shredded basil.

alcohol free	✔
citrus free	✔
dairy free	
gluten free	
wheat free	

spiced beef farfalle bake

Serves 6 – Preparation time: 10 minutes – Cooking time: 40 minutes

Per serving – Energy: 463 kcals/1954 kJ · Protein: 30 g · Carbohydrate: 56 g · Fat: 15 g · Fibre: 2 g

✔ alcohol free
✔ citrus free
dairy free
gluten free
wheat free

250 g	(8 oz) dried three-coloured farfalle
2	tablespoons oil
2	shallots, finely chopped
	pinch of ground cumin
1	dried chilli
250 g	(8 oz) minced lean beef
50–75 g	(2–3 oz) fresh coriander, chopped
425 g	(14 oz) can chickpeas, drained
425 g	(14 oz) can lentils, drained
2	tablespoons tomato purée
250 g	(8 oz) jar mesquite sauce
75 g	(3 oz) Emmental cheese, grated
	salt

Mesquite sauce is a hot, spicy sauce with a smoky flavour which comes from Mexico and Texas. It takes its name from the mesquite tree, which is used for smoking and barbecuing foods.

1 Bring a large pan of water to the boil. Add a generous pinch of salt. Cook the pasta according to packet instructions until just tender.

2 Meanwhile, heat the oil in a frying pan, add the shallots, cumin and chilli and fry for 2 minutes. Add the beef and fry over a high heat for 5 minutes, turning constantly. Stir in the chopped coriander, chickpeas, lentils, tomato purée and mesquite sauce, and simmer for 2 minutes.

3 Drain the pasta and return it to the saucepan. Stir the meat mixture into the pasta, then transfer it to a buttered 1.8 litre (3 pint) ovenproof dish. Sprinkle with the grated cheese and bake in a preheated oven at 180°C (350°F), Gas Mark 4 for 25 minutes.

chicken stew with couscous

Serves 4 – Preparation time: 30 minutes – Cooking time: 1¹/₂ hours

Per serving – Energy: 722 kcals/3020 kJ · Protein: 48 g · Carbohydrate: 76 g · Fat: 27 g · Fibre: 7 g

4	**tablespoons olive oil**
2	**onions, chopped**
1	**green or yellow pepper, cored, deseeded and chopped**
3	**tomatoes, skinned and chopped**
2	**red chillies, deseeded and finely chopped**
375 g	**(12 oz) turnips, quartered**
250 g	**(8 oz) small carrots, quartered**
3	**courgettes, sliced**
125 g	**(4 oz) fine green beans, topped and tailed**
1	**teaspoon ground coriander**
1	**teaspoon ground cumin**
1.5 kg	**(3 lb) chicken, jointed**
600 ml	**(1 pint) hot water**
250 g	**(8 oz) cooked or canned chickpeas**
375 g	**(12 oz) couscous**
25 g	**(1 oz) butter, diced**
	salt
	pepper

Hot Sauce:

2	**tablespoons tomato purée**
¹/₂–1	**teaspoon ready-made harissa paste**

alcohol free	✔
citrus free	✔
dairy free	
gluten free	
wheat free	

1 Heat the oil in a large heavy-based saucepan over a moderate heat and fry the onions, pepper, tomatoes and chillies for 5–6 minutes until soft. Add the turnips, carrots, courgettes and beans and stir well. Add the spices, chicken pieces, measured hot water, and salt and pepper to taste. Simmer gently for 20 minutes.

2 Add the chickpeas to the chicken mixture and simmer for 20–30 minutes more.

3 Meanwhile, soak the couscous in a bowl of cold water for 10–15 minutes, then stir gently with a wooden spoon to break up any lumps. Drain in a colander. Line a steamer with muslin and tip in the couscous.

4 Put the steamer containing the couscous over the pan with the chicken (it should not touch the stew below) and steam gently for about 15–20 minutes. Season the couscous to taste and gently break up any lumps. Dot with butter.

5 To make the hot sauce, take a couple of ladlefuls of liquid from the chicken stew and mix with the tomato purée and harissa. Serve the stew with the couscous and add the hot sauce separately.

poached figs with cassis in cinnamon sauce

Serves 4 – Preparation time: 10 minutes, plus cooling – Cooking time: 25 minutes

Per serving – Energy: 246 kcals/1036 kJ · Protein: 5 g · Carbohydrate: 27 g · Fat: 4 g · Fibre: 3 g

alcohol free	
✔	citrus free
dairy free	
✔	gluten free
✔	wheat free

300 ml	**('/₂ pint) red wine**
150 ml	**('/₄ pint) cassis**
2	**cinnamon sticks**
2	**strips of lemon rind**
2	**strips of orange rind**
300 ml	**('/₂ pint) water**
12	**large ripe firm figs, washed**
	Cinnamon Sauce:
150 g	**(5 oz) Greek yogurt**
2	**tablespoons clear honey**
1	**teaspoon ground cinnamon**

1 Place the wine, cassis, cinnamon sticks, citrus rind and water in a saucepan and bring to the boil.

2 Add the figs, cover the pan and simmer gently for 10 minutes until the figs are dark red and softened. Do not overcook or the figs will fall apart.

3 Remove the figs with a slotted spoon and place in a serving dish. Bring the poaching liquid to a rolling boil and simmer until it is reduced by half and is thick and syrupy. Pour over the figs and leave to cool.

4 Meanwhile, combine all the sauce ingredients and set aside to allow the flavours to develop. Serve the figs at room temperature with a spoonful of sauce for each serving.

peach, apricot and blueberry gratin

Serves 6 – Preparation time: 10 minutes, plus cooling – Cooking time: 5–6 minutes

Per serving – Energy: 308 kcals/1284 kJ · Protein: 6 g · Carbohydrate: 26 g · Fat: 21 g · Fibre: 3 g

4	**firm ripe peaches, halved, stoned and very thinly sliced**
6	**firm apricots, halved, stoned and very thinly sliced**
175 g	**(6 oz) blueberries**
250 g	**(8 oz) mascarpone cheese**
250 g	**(8 oz) Greek yogurt**
3	**tablespoons light muscovado sugar**
1	**teaspoon ground cinnamon**

1 Spoon the peaches, apricots and blueberries into a gratin dish.

2 Beat together the mascarpone and yogurt and spread over the fruit.

3 Combine the sugar and cinnamon and sprinkle over the surface to cover. Place under a preheated hot grill for 5–6 minutes until the sugar is caramelized. Leave to cool for a few minutes before serving.

alcohol free	✔
citrus free	✔
dairy free	
gluten free	✔
wheat free	✔

fruit malt loaf

Makes 1 small loaf – Preparation time: 10 minutes, plus rising – Cooking time: 45 minutes
8 slices, per slice – Energy: 167 kcals/711 kJ · Protein: 3 g · Carbohydrate: 33 g · Fat: 3 g · Fibre: 1 g

✔	alcohol free
✔	citrus free
	dairy free
✔	gluten free
✔	wheat free

15 g	(½ oz) dried yeast
75 ml	(3 fl oz) tepid water
1	teaspoon clear honey
125 g	(4 oz) brown rice flour
125 g	(4 oz) rye flour
125 g	(4 oz) sultanas
25 g	(1 oz) margarine
50 g	(2 oz) malt extract
25 g	(1 oz) black treacle
1	tablespoon clear honey, to glaze

1 Grease a 500 g (1 lb) loaf tin. Mix together the yeast, water and honey and leave in a warm place until frothy.

2 Mix together the flours and sultanas in a warm bowl. Put the margarine, malt extract and black treacle in a saucepan and heat gently until the margarine has melted. Leave to cool for 5 minutes.

3 Add the yeast and treacle to the dry ingredients and mix to a soft dough. Transfer to the loaf tin, cover with a damp cloth and leave for about 1 hour, or until doubled in size.

4 Bake the loaf in a preheated oven at 200°C (400°F), Gas Mark 6 for 45 minutes. Turn out on to a wire rack, brush with honey, then leave to cool.

tipsy fruit

Serves 4 – Preparation time: 15 minutes – Cooking time: 25 minutes
Per serving – Energy: 618 kcals/2620 kJ · Protein: 11 g · Carbohydrate: 12 g · Fat: 4 g · Fibre: 3 g

	alcohol free
	citrus free
	dairy free
✔	gluten free
✔	wheat free

450 ml	(¾ pint) sweet white wine
12	large prunes
12	dried figs
12	dried apple rings
8	dried apricots
	pared rind of ½ orange, cut into thin strips
	Apricot Cheese:
250 g	(8 oz) dried apricots
1	cinnamon stick
150 ml	(¼ pint) orange juice
125 g	(4 oz) fromage frais

1 Pour the wine into a saucepan and boil until reduced by half. Place in a large heatproof bowl with the fruit and cover with a piece of kitchen foil as a lid. Place in a steamer and set over a large pan of boiling water. Steam for 10 minutes.

2 Meanwhile, make the apricot cheese. Place the apricots, cinnamon and orange juice in a cup made of kitchen foil, then seal the edges together carefully. Place in the steamer with the fruit and steam for 10 minutes.

3 Remove the cinnamon stick. Put the apricots, orange juice and fromage frais in a food processor or blender and work until smooth. Blanch the orange rind in the steamer for 20 seconds. Cool in cold water.

4 Divide the apricot cheese between 4 plates. Arrange the fruit on top and decorate with strips of orange rind.

baked lemon and bay custards

Serves 8 – Preparation time: 5 minutes, plus infusing and cooling – Cooking time: 55–60 minutes

Per serving – Energy: 208 kcals/850 kJ · Protein: 4 g · Carbohydrate: 20 g · Fat: 12 g · Fibre: 0 g

12	**bay leaves, bruised**
2	**tablespoons grated lemon rind**
150 ml	**(¹/₄ pint) double cream**
4	**eggs**
1	**egg yolk**
150 g	**(5 oz) caster sugar**
100 ml	**(3¹/₂ fl oz) lemon juice**

This recipe is a variation of the classic lemon tart. Here, the lemon custard is infused with bay leaves, giving it a heady scent. The custard is baked in a very low oven: if the oven is too hot the custard will curdle. Check after 40 minutes to see if the custards are done – the centres should be almost set but still move a little. They will firm up as they cool.

1 Put the bay leaves, lemon rind and cream into a small saucepan and heat gently until it reaches boiling point. Remove from the heat and set aside for 2 hours to infuse.

2 Whisk together the eggs, egg yolk and sugar until the mixture is pale and creamy then whisk in the lemon juice. Strain the cream mixture through a fine sieve into the egg mixture and stir until combined.

3 Pour the custard into 8 individual ramekins and place on a baking sheet. Bake in a preheated oven at 120°C (250°F), Gas Mark ¹/₂ for 50 minutes, or until the custards are almost set in the middle. Leave until cold and chill until required. Return the custards to room temperature before serving.

alcohol free	✔
citrus free	
dairy free	
gluten free	✔
wheat free	✔

glossary

AURA: symptoms such as blurred or tunnel vision or neurological symptoms which occur before the headache of a migraine with aura begins.

ALLERGY: response or reaction set off by immune system when it comes into contact with food or other substance.

ALLERGEN: food or substance that triggers an allergic reaction.

NEUROTRANSMITTER: chemicals in the brain that send messages back and forth between brain cells.

NSAID: non-steroidal anti-inflammatory. Medications which reduce the effects of prostaglandins and reduce pain and inflammation.

SEROTONIN: chemical released by platelets in the bloodstream which constrict arteries. Serotonin also acts as a neurotransmitter.

PHOTOPHOBIA: dislike of bright light.

PHONOPHOBIA: dislike of noise.

PROSTAGLANDINS: chemicals that pass on pain signals to the brain. They also cause inflammation in the surrounding tissue.

ANALGESIC: medications that are used to reduce/relieve pain, ie painkillers. The term is often used in relation to painkillers that can be bought over the counter, such as aspirin, paracetamol and ibuprofen, but also refers to more potent medications including narcotics and anaesthetics.

CT SCAN: computerised tomography is a diagnostic technique that involves combined use of a computer and X-rays passed through the body at different angles to produce clear cross-sectional images of the tissue. It provides clearer and more detailed information than X-rays alone. It is often used for head and brain scans.

ENDORPHINS: naturally occurring chemicals that are found throughout the nervous system and appear to reduce pain. They are often referred to as 'the body's own painkillers.'

GLUTEN: a special protein found in wheat flour. Coeliac disease, which affects the small intestine, results when a person cannot digest gluten, while gluten sensitivity may result in headache or other conditions such as dermatitis.

MRI: magnetic resonance imaging is another type of diagnostic scanning technique but does not involve the use of X-rays or radiation. It is especially useful in obtaining images of the brain and spinal cord because it picks out white and grey matter. It is also useful to image soft tissue.

NOCICEPTORS: special sensory nerve endings that transmit pain signals and sensations.

VASCULAR: relating to the blood vessels. In certain types of headache and especially migraine, the pain may be the result of the blood vessels constricting (becoming smaller) or dilating (becoming larger).

useful addresses

Migraine Action Association
178a High Road
Byfleet
West Byfleet
Surrey KT14 7ED
Tel: 01932 352468
Website: www.migraine.org.uk

The Migraine Trust
45 Great Ormond Street
London WC1N 3HZ
020 7831 4818

ACUPUNCTURE

British Acupuncture Council
63 Jeddo Road, London W12 9HQ
Tel: 020 8735 0400
Website: www.acupuncture.org.uk

ALEXANDER TECHNIQUE

Society of Teachers of the Alexander Technique
20 London House, 266 Fulham Road,
London SW10 9EL
Tel: 020 7351 0828

AROMATHERAPY

Aromatherapy Organisations Council
PO Box 19834, London SE25 6WF
Tel: 020 8251 7912
Website: www.aromatherapy-uk.org

CHINESE MEDICINE

Register of Chinese Herbal Medicine
PO Box 400, Wembley, Middlesex HA9 9NZ
Tel: 020 7470 8740

CHIROPRACTIC

British Chiropractic Association
29 Whitley Street
Reading, Berks RG2 0EG

HOMOEOPATHY

The Society of Homoeopaths
4a Artizan Road, Northampton NN1 4HU
Tel: 01604 621400

OSTEOPATHY

British School of Osteopathy
275 Borough High Street, London SE1 1JE
Tel: 020 74070222
Website: www.bso.ac.uk

REFLEXOLOGY

Association of Reflexologists
27 Old Gloucester Street
London WC1N 3XX
Tel: 0870 5673320

WESTERN HERBALISM

National Institute of Medical Herbalists
56 Longbrooke Street, Exeter, EX4 6AH
Tel: 01392 426022

glossary and useful addresses

index

A

abdominal migraine, 21
abscesses, 18
accidents, post-traumatic
    headache, 17
acupressure, 53
acupuncture, 52
acute treatments, 42–3
adrenaline, 36
alcohol, as trigger, 29
Alexander Technique, 60
allergies, 66–9
amines, 64–6, 68
analgesics, 40–3, 65
aneurysm, 18
antidepressants, 44
antiemetics, 43
apples:
    rhubarb, apple and double
        ginger crumble, 92
aromatherapy, 56
asparagus roasted with
        coriander and lime, 76
aspirin, 16, 40, 65
aura, migraine, 19, 20, 21

B

Bach flower remedies, 57
banana shake, 96
basilar artery migraine, 21
beans:
    Caribbean black-eyed beans
        and rice, 84
    chilli bean and pepper soup, 72
beef:
    spiced beef farfalle bake, 118
    steak with fresh tomato sauce,
        80
beta blockers, 44
blood sugar levels, 30, 33, 37, 66
blood vessels, 10–11
    cluster headaches, 15
    migraine, 12
brain, 10
brain tumours, 18
bread:
    soda bread, 79
    walnut and sultana bread, 79
breakfast, 66, 96–7
bulgar wheat with tomato, broad
        beans, feta and mint, 108

C

Caesar salad, 98
caffeine, 16, 41, 64, 65
carbohydrates, 66

Caribbean black-eyed beans and
        rice, 84
Champagne summer berries, 91
cheese:
    herb salad with grilled haloumi,
        77
    mozzarella and plum tomato
        lasagne with chilli, 116
    spinach and goats' cheese
        salad, 103
Chi, 52, 53
chicken:
    chicken and broccoli risotto,
        83
    chicken and raisin salad, 100
    chicken-filled tortillas, 82
    chicken kebabs and marinated
        rice, 81
    chicken stew with couscous,
        119
    smoked chicken and citrus
        salad, 100
chicken liver salad, 77
chickpea, pasta and spinach
        soup, 107
chicory:
    chicory and pear salad, 99
    chicory, orange and pasta
        salad, 101
chilli bean and pepper soup, 72
chilli tagliatelle, 85
Chinese herbalism, 50
chiropractic, 54
chronic daily headache, 15–16
chronic tension-type headaches,
        14
cluster headaches, 15
cod:
    sweet and sour cod cutlets,
        112
    Thai steamed fish curry, 110
codeine, 16, 41
complementary therapies, 47–61
compresses, 37
contraceptive pills, 30, 31
copper, 68
couscous:
    chicken stew with, 119
    green lentil and vegetable
        tagine with, 115
curry, Thai steamed fish, 110
custards, baked lemon and bay,
        123

D

dehydration, 66

diary, of triggers, 26–7
diet, 28, 63–9
doctors, 22–3
drugs:
    chronic daily headache, 15–16
    painkillers, 40–3
    preventative treatment, 44–5

E

Eastern therapies, 52–3
eating habits, as trigger, 29–30
encephalitis, 18
endorphins, 12
environmental triggers, 34–5
episodic tension-type
        headaches, 13
ergotamine, 15, 16, 42
essential oils, 56, 57
exclusion diet, 69, 71
exercise, 33–4, 37
exertion headache, 16–17

F

fava, 73
fettuccine with chanterelles, 84
feverfew, 51
figs poached with cassis, 120
fish cakes, tuna, 105
fish oil, 67
flower remedies, 57
food, 28, 63–9
food additives, 65
food allergy and intolerance, 66–9
fruit:
    Champagne summer berries,
        91
    spiced fruit compôte, 96
    tipsy fruit, 122
fruit malt loaf, 122

G

ginger, 67
green bean and vegetable soup
        with pesto, 106
"

H

halibut:
    baked halibut with rosemary,
        87
    halibut aurora, 86
hangovers, 29
headaches:
    causes, 10
    complementary therapies,
        47–61
    food and, 63–9

managing, 37
orthodox medicines, 39–45
symptoms, 10
triggers, 26–36
types, 13–19
hemiplegic migraine, 21
herb salad with grilled haloumi,
        77
herbalism, 50–1
histamine, 15, 65, 68
homoeopathy, 56
hormones:
    oestrogen, 21, 31, 32
    stress hormones, 36
    as trigger, 30–1
HRT (hormone replacement
        therapy), 30, 32

I

ibuprofen, 41
immune system, 68
insomnia, 33

K

kedgeree, 104

L

lamb salad with minted yogurt,
        99
lasagne:
    mozzarella and plum tomato
        lasagne with chilli, 116
lavender oil, 57
lemon:
    baked lemon and bay custards,
        123
    lemon pudding, 91
lentils:
    green lentil and vegetable
        tagine with couscous, 115

M

malt loaf, 122
manipulation, 54–5
massage, 55
meditation, 59
meningitis, 18
menopause, 30, 32
menstrual migraine, 21, 30–1
menstruation, 30–1
meridians, 52, 53
migraine:
    causes, 12
    chronic daily headache, 16
    managing, 37
    menstrual migraine, 21, 30–1

pain, 18
phases of an attack, 20
symptoms, 10, 12, 18–19
triggers, 12, 26–36
minerals, 66–7
mixed leaf salad, 75
monosodium glutamate (MSG), 65
morels with wild rice, 89
movement therapies, 60–1
mozzarella and plum tomato lasagne with chilli, 116
muesli, oaty, 97
mushrooms:
    fettuccine with chanterelles, 84
    morels with wild rice, 89

N
natural therapies, 56–7
nausea, 12, 43
nerves, 10, 11
    migraine, 12
    pain receptors, 11
neurotransmitters, 12
niacin, 67
nitrates, 65
nitrites, 65
nocioceptors, 11, 12
noodles in spicy broth, 104
NSAIDs (non steroidal anti-inflammatory drugs), 41, 43
nutritional deficiencies, 66–7

O
oaty muesli, 97
oestrogen, 21, 31, 32
oils, essential, 56, 57
ophthalmoplegic migraine, 21
opioids, 16
organic headaches, 18
osteopathy, 55

P
pain, 10
    cluster headaches, 15
    mechanism of, 11–12
    migraine, 18
    tension-type headaches, 13
painkillers, 15–16, 40–3, 65
pappardelle with pesto and potatoes, 85
paracetamol, 16, 40, 65
pasta primavera, 109
peach, apricot and blueberry gratin, 121

pears:
    chicory and pear salad
    pear and cardamom flan, 93
pepper sauce, baked pasta with, 117
phenylethylamine, 65
pizotifen, 45
pizza, many tomato, 88
plaice:
    stuffed fillets of fish with stir-fried vegetables, 113
platelets, 12, 40, 67
pork in hot sauce, 81
post-traumatic headache, 17
posture, 34
potatoes:
    breakfast squeak, 97
    new potato salad, 74
    pappardelle with pesto and potatoes, 85
pre-eclampsia, 32
pregnancy, 30, 31–2
premenstrual headache, 16
prostaglandins, 40, 41, 43

R
rebound headache, 15–16, 41
reflexology, 55
relaxation, 58–9
retinal migraine, 21
rhubarb, apple and double ginger crumble, 92
rice:
    kedgeree, 104
    rice with coconut milk, 90
    vegetable biryani, 114
risotto, chicken and broccoli, 83

S
salads, 74–7, 98–103
serotonin, 12, 21, 32, 42, 44, 51
serotonin antagonists, 45
sexual headache, 17
shiatsu, 53
sinus headache, 16
skull, 10
sleep, 33, 37
smoked haddock:
    kedgeree, 104
    smoked haddock chowder, 74
soda bread, 79
sole:
    lemon sole with oranges and rice, 112
soups, 72, 74
spinach and goats' cheese salad,

103
spinal cord, posture, 34
stabbing headache, 18
strawberry and melon cups, 97
stress, 35–6
stroke, 17, 18
sumatriptan, 42
supplements, 67
synephrine, 65

T
tagliatelle, chilli, 85
Tense Release, 58
tension, 35–6
tension-type headaches, 11, 13–14
Thai steamed fish curry, 110
therapists, 48–9
tomatoes:
    many tomato pizza, 88
tortillas, chicken-filled, 82
transformed migraine, 16
travel, 36
triggers, 12, 26–36, 64–9
trout:
    rainbow trout with lemon and ginger stuffing, 111
tumours, brain, 18
tuna fish cakes, 105
tyramine, 64–6

V
vascular headaches, 11
vasoactive amines, 64–5, 68
vegetables:
    pasta primavera, 109
    roasted autumn vegetables, 78
    vegetable biryani, 114
visual disturbances, migraine, 19, 20
visualization, 58
vitamins, 66–7
vomiting, 12, 43

W
walnut and sultana bread, 79
weather, 34–5
weekend headaches, 36
Western herbalism, 51
whiplash injury, 17
wine, as trigger, 29
winter radish salad, 102

Y
yellow split peas, fava, 73
yoga, 61

index

FRONT COVER

Tony Stone/Rosanne Olson Front Cover top

BACK COVER

Tony Stone/Rosanne Olson

Bridgeman Art Library/Geoffrey Museum 6

Bubbles/Loisjoy Thurston 31

Octopus Publishing Group Ltd./Colin Bowling 51 Top, 51 Bottom /Jean Cazals 29 Bottom /Laurie Evans 64 /Colin Gotts 60 Bottom /Graham Kirk 65, 69 Bottom /Sandra Lane 19, 26 Bottom, 29 Top /Gary Latham 7 left, 14, 33 Bottom /Peter Myers 28, 34, 59 Bottom /Bill Reavell 5 Top, 5 Top Centre Right, 30 Bottom, 46, 48 Top, 50 Top, 52 Top, 54 Top, 56 Top, 58 Top, 60 Top, 62, 68 Top /Ian Wallace 21, 69 Top /Mark Winwood 55 Bottom

Robert Harding Picture Library 35, 36 Top /Barry Elz 13 /Giovanni Lunardi 33 Top

Image Bank/David de Lossy 43

Photodisc 4 Top, 56 Bottom, 57, 59 Top, 67 Top, 67 Centre, 67 Bottom, 68 Centre, 68 Bottom

Science Photo Library/Oscar Burriel 4 Top Centre Right, 8 left, 10, 22 /Scott Camazine 16 /Dagmar Ehling 54 /Erich Schremp 11 right /Mark de Fraeye 53 Bottom /Tim Malyn/Paul Biddle 52 Bottom, 53 Top /Mehau Kulyk 11 left /Oscar Burriel/ Latin Stoc 12 /CC Studio 23 /Hattie Young 55 Top /Saturn Stills 50 Bottom

Tony Stone Images/Victoria Blacki 4 Bottom, 38, 40, 42, 44 /Jon Bradley 15 /Peter Cade 49 /James Darell 4 Bottom Centre Right, 24, 37 /Deborah Denker 41 /Deborah Jaffe 17 /Tony May 30 Top /Laurence Monneret 32 /Rosanne Olson 1 /Andre Perlstein 36 Bottom /Joe Polollio 45 /Jon Riley 7 right /David Rosenberg 61 /Timothy Shonnard 26 Top

Safety Note

Food Solutions: Headaches and Migraines should not be considered a replacement for professional medical treatment; a physician should be consulted in all matters relating to health, particularly in respect of pregnancy and any symptoms which may require diagnosis or medical attention. While the advice and information in this book is believed to be accurate, neither the author nor publisher can accept any legal responsibility for any injury or illness sustained while following the treatments and diet plan.

acknowledgements